Meaningless Words
& *Broken* Covenants

How Our Words
and the Agreements Built on Them
are Becoming Increasingly
MEANINGLESS

Tim Coody

TATE PUBLISHING, LLC

"Meaningless Words and Broken Covenants: How Our Words and the Agreements Built on Them are Becoming Increasingly Meaningless" by Tim Coody

Copyright © 2006 by Tim Coody. All rights reserved.

Published in the United States of America
by Tate Publishing, LLC
127 East Trade Center Terrace
Mustang, OK 73064
(888) 361-9473

Book design copyright © 2006 by Tate Publishing, LLC. All rights reserved.

No part of this publication may be reproduced, stored in a retrieval system or transmitted in any way by any means, electronic, mechanical, photocopy, recording or otherwise without the prior permission of the author except as provided by USA copyright law.

All scriptural quotations are from the NIV unless otherwise noted. Taken from the *Holy Bible, New International Version* ®, Copyright © 1973, 1978, 1984 by International Bible Society. Used by permission of Zondervan Publishing House. All rights reserved.

Scripture quotations marked "TAB" are taken from *The Amplified Bible, Old Testament,* Copyright © 1965, 1987 by the Zondervan Corporation and *The Amplified New Testament,* Copyright © 1958, 1987 by The Lockman Foundation. Used by permission. All rights reserved.

Scripture quotations marked "KJV" are taken from the *Holy Bible, King James Version*, Cambridge, 1769.

This book is designed to provide accurate and authoritative

information with regard to the subject matter covered. This information is given with the understanding that neither the author nor Tate Publishing, LLC is engaged in rendering legal, professional advice. Since the details of your situation are fact dependent, you should additionally seek the services of a competent professional.

Although many of the stories in this book have been based on actual case histories, names, places, and other entities may have been changed or have been changed to protect the confidentiality and privacy of all parties involved.

ISBN: 1-5988624-6-4

Acknowledgments

The Lord works in such subtle and humble ways that He seldom leaves a fingerprint. I asked Him to write this book through me each time I sat down to work on it. I don't say this to bully you into agreeing with the positions that I put forward. I say it simply to acknowledge and thank Him for His assistance.

My wife Laura's organizational skills and support played a major role in turning interesting ideas about words into a book. Her willingness to give me honest feedback was a blessing and helped to keep me on track. Laura and our girls, Hannah and Katherine, allowed me the time needed to work on this project, and I appreciate their love, patience, and support.

Tim McKeown's encouragement, advice, and journalistic skill were instrumental in getting this project off the ground and keeping it in the air. It's amazing what a good encourager can do. My brother Bret's insight, advice, and proofreading skills were very helpful. His eye can catch an error that few will ever find. The hours he spent proofreading the manuscript will always be appreciated. Rita Holland's keen Biblical insight and honest feedback were very helpful and much appreciated. Many friends and family members have been a great source of encouragement throughout the process, and I appreciate their encouragement and prayers.

Foreword

The honoring of the marital covenant between God and husbands and wives is at the heartbeat of God. Yet we live in a culture that is breaking God's heart as well as children and spouses' when covenants aren't honored. Tim Coody has done a remarkable job at focusing on the Word of God and His passion around His covenant with each of us. Read this book with a teachable heart, search the Bible to understand His Truth about covenant, and purpose to serve Him by honoring your marriage covenant. Your legacy will carry the blessing for generations to come.

    Dr. Gary Rosberg, President
    America's Family Coaches
    Author of *Divorce Proof Your Marriage*

TABLE OF CONTENTS

Introduction 13

Chapter 1 21
Meaninglessness (*A Deadly Epidemic*)

Chapter 2 25
Heart and Mouth Disease

Chapter 3 31
Lying, Satan's Native Language (*Symptom #1*)

Chapter 4 43
Empty Words (*Symptom #2*)

Chapter 5 49
Damaged Relationships (*Symptom #3*)

Chapter 6 57
Self-control Problems (*Symptom #4*)

Chapter 7 63
Inability to Connect with God (*Symptom #5*)

Chapter 8 69
Broken Vows (*Symptom #6*)

Chapter 9 .... **75**
Covenants

Chapter 10 .... **81**
Our Covenant with Christ

Chapter 11............................. **87**
The Marriage Covenant

Chapter 12 .... **95**
Why Christians Ignore Marriage Covenants

Chapter 13 .... **107**
Self on the Cross or on the Run?

Chapter 14 .... **113**
The Consequences of Broken Covenants

Chapter 15 .... **121**
Damage to the Godly Seed

Chapter 16 .... **129**
Exposing the Sin

Chapter 17 .... **137**
Why Not Repent?

Chapter 18 .... **143**
How Can I Ever Untangle This Mess?

Chapter 19 .... **147**
Redemption

Bibliography............................ **157**

Introduction

Imagine waking up one morning in a strange world–like Bill Murray in the movie *Ground Hog Day*–but with a twist. Instead of repeating the same day, as in the movie, you live a day in which words have no meaning at all. The words seem to mean something when you say them, and people appear to respond to them. But no evidence indicates that your words, or anyone's words for that matter, are to be taken seriously.

You contact your broker and ask him to sell a plummeting stock. He agrees to make the deal, but you find out later that day that no record of the call exists. On the way to work you order an Egg McMuffin. The girl at the window takes your money but gives you a hot fudge sundae. You confront her about the mistake, and she apologizes profusely. After waiting, confident that the problems have been resolved, she opens the window, smiles a friendly smile, and hands you a container of orange juice.

Nothing stated has any meaning, just empty words that make familiar noises but carry no reliable message. Things don't get any better when you show up at work. The workday turns into a series of confusing interactions that leave you totally perplexed, unsure of any communication that takes place all day. At the end of the day, you pull into your driveway, confident that the madness is finally over. Your wife listens attentively as you go over the bizarre details of the day; she nods her head knowingly in agreement as you talk. Finally! The sense of relief is almost palpable, and you thank her for listening and tell her you love her. But she yawns and walks away as if nothing of any significance has been conveyed. The door suddenly slams, jarring you out of your sense of confusion. The kids are running and screaming through the house. You tell them to be quiet, and they stop long enough to respectfully agree to your request, and then almost instantly return to the same noisy games.

The stress builds as you begin to wonder if you're living an old episode of The Twilight Zone. Food seems to help at stressful times like this, but you remember your New Year's resolution and the promises you made to yourself to stay on the diet. Those memories fade as quickly as they appeared, and you stuff yourself like there is no tomorrow. Oh no! Now you're struck with the frightening realization that even the words you tell yourself are worthless. They are all meaningless.

Whew, what a nightmare! Can you imagine the torment of it? What if the tools you use to interface with reality—your words—lost their ability to transport meaning? The social currents are pulling us in that direction today, a place where words are losing their meaning and the agreements built on them are crumbling.

To get a feel for it, imagine yourself behind the wheel of an ice racer on a frozen lake. You stomp the gas pedal to the floor when the starter waves the flag. The engine roars, but you're not going anywhere. Instead of spiked tires ripping into the ice, you're polishing the ice with bald tires. No problem with power, but you can't seem to apply it to the icy surface. Finally, you manage to pull away from the start line and build some momentum, but the first turn reminds you of what happened at the start line. You turn the wheel but no response. The car slides off the track. The brakes are no help either with bald tires, and you brace for impact with the approaching barrier.

What a mess. But that is a picture of what life is like for many people today. Like tires contacting the pavement, words interface with our reality. If they grip well, communication with self and others becomes relatively predictable. But what happens when words begin to lose their grip? Many of our words, even our most important words, don't mean what they used to. Our words are worn out. From the simple, "Tell them I'm not in the office right now," to the solemn, "Till death do we part," our words are losing their grip. The tread is disappearing, and the meaning is leaking out.

Let me give you a more tangible example. A recent article in *Christianity Today* reported some alarming statistics about the True Love Waits campaign. In his article entitled "The Scandal of the Evangelical Conscience," Ronald J. Sider sites research that followed 12,000 young people who took the True Love Waits pledge over a seven-year period. Eighty-eight percent of the young people who pledged to wait admitted that they had engaged in sexual intercourse prior to marriage. Sadly, only 12 percent of this group kept their promise.

Eighty-eight percent of these teens solemnly pledged that they would not have sex before marriage, but they did. Hormones and social pressures faced off against honor and integrity. The final score was "88 to 12." The home team lost. Honor and integrity will have to spend a little more time in the gym if they want victory anytime soon.

How did these kids learn that their words could be ignored just as if they had never been spoken? Why did Jane's "I promise to remain celibate" surrender to Billy's hormonal "I'll always love you" in the heat of the moment? The reason is because Jane's promise to remain celibate prior to marriage carried no more weight than Billy's promise to always love her. The final exam was held in the back seat of Billy's car on a Friday night, and neither passed.

A growing trend to disregard our words and commitments is emerging. A reflection of this trend is evident in the rapid rise in the number of lawyers in this country; their numbers tripled between 1960 and 1990. Why would one occupation need to triple in thirty years? Hosea knew the answer to that question eight centuries before Christ. "They make many promises, take false oaths and make agreements; therefore lawsuits spring up like poisonous weeds in a plowed field" (Hosea 10:4). We needed more lawyers because we started suing each other more often. After 1969 and no-fault divorce, we started suing each other a lot more often. We started suing each other more often because we could not keep our agreements. We could not keep our agreements because we forgot the importance of honoring our words. Without honor in our words everything falls apart sooner or later.

Have you noticed how many words it takes to make a simple agreement these days? My apartment lease in 1978 was one page. You would be hard pressed to find one less than ten pages today. We use more words now than we did in 1978 to do the same job. All these words assure us that people will keep their agreements–right? Wrong. As Solomon said, "The more the words, the less the meaning, and how does that profit anyone?" (Eccles. 6:11). We are drowning in a sea of words. But with the abundance of the noise comes a dearth of meaning.

My insurance policy states, "Carefully read your policy." Who has time to carefully read their policy? My auto insurance policy alone covers thirty-nine pages, a small book of boring legalities. If I was a more responsible policy holder I would read every word, right after I finished with the dishwasher warranty, but I'm not.

In the Old West people didn't have to worry

about insurance so much. If somebody fell down in the church lobby, they didn't sue. They just got up. They didn't lie so much back then either. Watch an old Western from the 1960s when you have some spare time. Calling a cowboy a liar was a great way to get shot. Even in 1964 when I was watching black and white TV, it was still a big deal to call anyone a liar.

But after Monica Lewinski, all that changed. People were calling the President of the United States a liar. This is what President Clinton said at a news conference on March 8, 1998: "I am going to say this again: I did not have sexual relations with that woman, Miss Lewinsky." Later that year President Clinton was still in a lot of hot water over the whole affair. He testified before the Grand Jury stating: "It depends on what the meaning of the word 'is' is. If the–if he–if 'is' means is and never has been, that is not–that is one thing. If it means there is none, that was a completely true statement." This was the leader of the free world. The people who held the signs that said "It's the economy, stupid!" put him in office. But we found out that some things are more important than even the economy.

Numerous Biblical illustrations show us how differently men once viewed their words. Isaac is a great example. Why did Isaac refuse to change the blessing that he mistakenly gave to Jacob? Couldn't he have said "You tricked me . . . Because of your lies I will change the blessing I gave you and give it to Esau?" The Bible says that when Isaac found out he had been deceived he "trembled violently" (Gen. 27:33). Nevertheless, he didn't change a thing. Isaac viewed his words as if set in stone from the moment they left his mouth. Strong emotions–anger, betrayal, and disappointment–had no effect on his blessing to Jacob. That is a strange notion for us today. Can you imagine a man like Isaac holding a sign that read "It's the economy, stupid!"? He would be appalled by the dismal lack of integrity now present in our words.

In Biblical times, even the godless kept their word, and at great personal expense. Take the Old Testament example of King Darius. Because of his thoughtless decree, his friend Daniel was forced to go into the lion's den. The reason— "the laws of the Medes and Persians, which cannot be repealed" (Daniel 6:12). This king possessed great powers, but not the power to repeal his words in an effort to save his friend's life. Even this godless culture recognized the value of solid words and paid a high price to sustain them.

Herod Antipas is a New Testament example. His promise to his step-daughter led to the death of John the Baptist. He didn't want to order John's beheading, but he was trapped by his vow to do "whatever she asked" (Matt.14:7). You simply had to do what you said you would do in those times. What did these people know about words that we have tragically forgotten? They knew that when words are rendered meaningless, so is everything else. They courageously accepted the heavy toll required of honor and integrity to preserve meaningfulness in their lives. We have become unwilling to pay the high toll that honor demands, and now we must face the consequence–meaninglessness.

Time has changed the way we look at our words. We are more sophisticated now. We can change our words easily to protect us from the slightest inconvenience if necessary. Our words are no longer carefully considered and then chiseled in stone. They are mass-produced on word processors, and they come and go with the greatest of ease. There is only one problem. Our words are becoming meaningless.

Chapter 1
Meaninglessness
(A Deadly Epidemic)

False words are not only evil in themselves, but they infect the soul with evil.

—Plato

"Meaninglessness" is the name I've attached to this epidemic. I define it like this: a diseased state of the heart reflected by words that have no meaning; senseless communications. The words may be spoken aloud to others or silently affirmed to self. The intent to deceive is not a factor in the diagnosis. The issue is the accuracy, reliability, and truthfulness of the words themselves. This disease attacks words, draining the meaning out of them. Once empty, the words can no longer sustain meaningful relational or spiritual life. The attack is subtle, and the victim is often unaware of the problem until it is too late.

Diseases have stages they progress through. Meaninglessness is no exception. The stages are

21

described below.

The Stages of Meaninglessness:

1. Failure to keep mundane internal agreements: Deceit of self is the first warning that things are awry. The stated intent is to accomplish a task during the day, but obstacles appear that make it difficult to carry through, so it doesn't get done. This is not earth-shattering and creates little or no damage to relationships. It simply illustrates that intentions, represented by words, are beginning to slip.

2. Exaggeration: The willingness to make small alterations in the truth begins to appear here. This could be in the form of the simple exaggeration of a story. Most people believe it is completely harmless. It isn't. The damage to relationships remains relatively insignificant at this stage.

3. "Little white lies": "Tell them I'm not in the office right now . . . Tell them Daddy isn't home." The key damage occurs between the white liar and those involved in the deception–the secretary or the kids. The willingness to alter the truth and obtain accomplices in the process is an indication that integrity is slipping.

4. Lying: Tammy lies to colleagues, friends, and family about where she is, what she's doing, etc. When this is detected–and it will be–it can seriously damage the fabric of any relationship. Once it becomes accepted behavior with others, it becomes accepted behavior with herself. She doesn't know what the truth is any more.

5. *Promise breaking*: Dad promises the kids that they will all go fishing on Saturday, but a lucrative business opportunity wins out over his words. Sally promises her husband that she will never gamble again, but on payday she blows it all. Increasing levels of relational damage occur at this level to everyone involved. Trust is seriously damaged.

6. *Covenant breaking*: Bob files for divorce on Sharon. John walks away from his commitment to Christ and never turns back. The words "Till death do we part" and "Lord" have become meaningless. A covenant is "two becoming one," and covenant breaking seriously disrupts their sense of integrity.

7. *Self-Control and Addiction*: These issues can and do emerge prior to covenant breaking. These problems are always an indication that words of restraint are falling on deaf ears. Only God can rescue a person caught in the deeper levels of this trap because Meaninglessness has destroyed the person's ability to launch any kind of successful counterattack.

8. *Total Meaninglessness/Insanity*: Game's over, brother. Only a miracle can free a man from this cage. His words have lost all meaning. No one who knows

him trusts him. The habitual lies have eroded all of his relationships, and only the hollowed-out shells of old relationships remain, which are only meaningful in this person's deceived mind.

CHAPTER 2
Heart and Mouth Disease

For out of the overflow of the heart the mouth speaks.

—Matthew 12:34

Meaninglessness is a disease of the heart and mouth. *Vine's Expository Dictionary of Biblical Words* defines the heart as "man's entire mental and moral activity . . . used figuratively for the hidden springs of the personal life . . . the center of man's inward life." What does the heart have to do with our words, and why is the connection important? Three voices, two from the Bible and one from the world, will address these questions.

The first is the voice of Jesus, who makes several profound statements about the connection between our heart and our mouth in the book of Matthew.

> You brood of vipers, how can you who are evil say anything good? For out of the

overflow of the heart the mouth speaks. The good man brings good things out of the good stored up in him, and the evil man brings evil things out of the evil stored up in him. But I tell you that men will have to give account on the day of judgment for every careless word they have spoken. For by your words you will be acquitted, and by your words you will be condemned. (Matt.12:34–37)

There are three points of interest for our purposes. The first is "out of the overflow of the heart the mouth speaks" (Matt. 12:34). Jesus affirms the connection of two organs that otherwise seem totally disconnected–the heart and the mouth. I always thought that the mouth could function independently of the heart, but this is not what Jesus teaches. Sooner or later, in one form or another, what is in the heart will be exposed by the words that come out of the mouth. Most people have very limited control over what comes out of their mouth. Have you ever experienced the struggle between the juicy gossip and the promise not to tell within your heart? If so, you know the pressure that the springs of the heart can exert on the bounds of the mouth. The more filth in our heart creates more pressure to spew filth out of our mouth. The will struggles to cap the springs that flow out of the heart, especially if the words are ugly, but it can't stop them, according to Jesus. The Pharisees could not say anything good because their hearts were filthy. Jesus chose the word "heart" because it is more inclusive of everything happening above and below our conscious awareness. Certainly you have said things you had no intention of saying, most of which got you in trouble. We can't help it. Sooner or later what is in our heart will be out in the open with the help of our big fat mouth. To sum it up, the mouth speaks for the heart, not just the conscious mind.

The second point of interest deals with accountability. "Men will have to give account on the day of judgment for every careless word they have spoken." The word "careless" means "idle, unprofitable" (*The Complete WordStudy New Testament* 887). That sounds a lot like a meaningless word to me. We will each have to give an account of our careless, idle, and meaningless words. Not only will men give an account of every idle word, but the words have the power to acquit or condemn. "For by your words you will be acquitted, and by your words you will be condemned" (Matt. 12:37). It sounds like God is paying very close attention to our words even when we aren't.

The third point Jesus makes deals with a different scripture. "But the things that come out of the mouth come from the heart, and these make a man 'unclean'" (Matt.15:18). The Pharisees taught that what went into the mouth made a person unclean, but Jesus taught just the opposite. He said what came out of the mouth made a person unclean. The very act of uttering lies, slander, gossip, vulgarity, etc. has a defiling effect on us. The more we do it the more we want to do it.

In summary, Jesus said that what comes out of our mouth is very important, and we should be very careful to monitor it closely. Our mouth will expose exactly what's in our heart, and we won't be able to hide it. Secondly, we will be accountable for every word we speak. Finally, the act of speaking meaningless words defiles us. It makes us dirty and creates an urge to spew forth even more filth.

Solomon, the world's wisest man, also had a lot to say about words. He too was interested in the heart and mouth connection. "Above all else, guard your heart, for it is the wellspring of life" (Proverbs 4:23). Both Solomon and Jesus describe the heart as a kind of spring that pours out whatever resides in it. How does one guard his heart? The next verse answers the question. "Put away perversity from your mouth; keep corrupt talk far from your lips" (Prov. 4:24). Why are we told to guard it "above all else?" What is it that Solomon knew about words that we fail to grasp? *Solomon knew that words carry not only meaning, they transport life or death to our soul.* Consider that statement for just a moment before reading on. This is why this issue is such a big deal. Meaningless words are conceived in the chambers of our heart. They are not only created there, they circulate there and can cause serious damage. Something about the Word of God brings life and health to His children. *God employs words in some inscrutable way to actually carry and give us life.* They are precious containers that must be treated with care. Our heart too must be treated with care if it is to thrive and reproduce the gospel in others. James says it like this: "He chose to give us birth through the word of truth, that we might be a kind of firstfruits of all he created" (James 1:18). That is a profound thought. He gives us birth and maintains our life through His words. God places such significance upon His words because they carry spiritual life and health to our souls.

Meaningless words do damage to our heart as we listen, consider, and then speak them. We cannot see it or feel it, but the process of circulating meaningless words, lies, filth, and gossip through our heart defiles us. As the scripture says, "The words of a gossip are like choice morsels; they go down to a man's inmost parts" (Prov. 26:22). In some form, invisible to the naked eye (and to the MRI for that matter) the words of a gossip go down to a man's inmost parts. They go down into our heart. Then those same defiling words end up overflowing the bounds of our heart. Finally, they end up coming out of our mouth, and that's a problem.

To sum up Solomon's advice, guarding our heart should be a top priority. This comes about by keeping perverse speech out of our mouth. According to Solomon, the way we use our words is a matter of life and death. "The tongue has the power of life and death, and those who love it will eat its fruit" (Prov. 18:21).

We've heard what Jesus and Solomon had to say about Heart and Mouth Disease. Now it's time for the world's perspective on the problem. It can be summed up simply: words don't really matter any more. Character and integrity belong to the past; they are too inconvenient for busy people today. "It's the economy, stupid!" But the world must pay for the convenience of being able to ignore its words when they become hard to keep, and the price is a lonely, meaningless existence. Let's look at the symptoms of Meaninglessness.

Chapter 3
Lying, Satan's Native Language
(Symptom #1)

When he lies, he speaks his native language, for he is a liar and the father of lies.
—Jesus (John 8:44)

    Airports are great places to find different languages. People from around the globe mix, mingle, and communicate in airports. Recently, I heard the strangest language ever. Two travelers were behind me in a long security line speaking a language I had never heard before. Sometimes it sounded a little like Hebrew and at others it sounded almost Russian. My curiosity got the best of me, and I asked. They were nice enough to tell me a little about themselves. They were Jewish but grew up in Iran, and they were speaking a combination of Hebrew, Yiddish, and Farsi (the language of Iran).

According to the Bible, the Devil has also created a language of his own. He and his servants speak it fluently. When someone lies, you can know for sure where it originated. Jesus said this about the Devil, "When he lies, he speaks his native language . . ." (John 8:44).

Have you ever considered lying to be an actual language? According to the Bible it is. The evil one speaks it fluently. He and his people speak lies, listen to them, grow to love them, and then become ensnared by them.

Lying is both the gateway to, and a symptom of, Meaninglessness. It will always be present in some form with the disease. Some people have a strange attraction to lies; they prefer them to the truth. You may know somebody like that. Although God can clearly recognize a perverse heart without ever hearing it utter a deceitful word, men cannot. Lying is the first tangible evidence that a human being has the disease of Meaninglessness.

Lying bothered David a great deal. This is what he said about a liar named Doeg, "You love evil rather than good, falsehood rather than speaking the truth" (Psalm 52:3). Doeg isn't the only one who has this problem. Many people love evil more than good, and they love lying more than telling the truth. Isn't that amazing? David saw something about lying through the eyes of the Holy Spirit as he penned these inspired words. *He reveals that the liar develops a "love" for lying and actually prefers it to the truth!*

The mouth and tongue are strange body parts.

When we feed them poison, they want more. This happens in both the material and immaterial realms. For example, if you've ever tried beer, you know that it takes awhile to begin to like it. You have to develop a taste for it, but once the appetite is developed, some people can't seem to get enough. Even a case of beer (2.25 gallons) per day is not enough to satisfy some people's cravings.

The same is true with food. Someone overweight and with a heart condition shouldn't be eating cheesecake, but if they have learned to love it, guess what's for dessert? The same thing happens with lies, gossip, slander, and all other vile ways of using our mouth. Once the appetite for it develops, that's all the mouth wants to do.

It's not just the mouth that's involved. Once the lie is accepted as the currency of exchange, the ears start to get in on the act. "A wicked man listens to evil lips; a liar pays attention to a malicious tongue" (Prov. 17:4). This verse indicates that not only does the liar have an urge to speak lies; he also wants to listen to them. It's as if he has become fluent in the language of lying. Since that's his method of communication, he wants to spend time with others of a like mind, and he can't understand those who speak the truth. He can't understand why they get upset about his lies or why they work so hard to tell the truth when a lie would "solve" the problem so easily. He just doesn't love the truth.

In the book of Revelation, Jesus also acknowledges this strange phenomenon that people can actually come to love lies when He says, "Outside are the dogs, those who practice magic arts, the sexually immoral, the murderers, the idolaters and everyone who loves and practices falsehood" (Rev. 22:15). Like with alcohol, drugs, pornography, and gambling, the liar can't seem to let go of his lies, even though they get him into all sorts of trouble.

Letting go of something you've embraced is hard to do. Even monkeys have trouble with it. That's what makes them so easy to catch. Monkey trappers in North Africa take a hollowed-out gourd with a hole cut in the top just large enough for a monkey to stick his hand into. Then they chain the gourd to a tree and put some tasty nuts inside. When the curious monkey finds the gourd, he can barely get his empty hand through the hole. And when he grabs the nuts inside he can't get his clenched fist out of the gourd. The monkey can't let go of his "treasure" even when the trappers show up to check the traps. Isn't that amazing? He clings to the nuts and in the process loses his life. Liars are a lot like those monkeys. They'll hold on to their lies at the cost of their friendships, their marriages, and their lives. Isn't that bizarre? But it's true.

How does the liar come to a place where they want to speak and listen to lies? Why does this happen? The Bible makes it clear. "They perish because they refused to love the truth and so be saved" (II Thes. 2:10). This verse reveals the fact that some people don't love the truth. Their choice not to love the truth carries some heavy consequences. The soul is much like a vacuum tank. If the truth is not near the intake, it will suck up the only alternative–lies. People who choose not to love the truth and surround themselves with it, will end up full of lies. Without a love of the truth, lies will take control of the person's life. It's simply a matter of time. Loving and valuing the truth is the only protection from lies. To love the truth is to hate lying, and to live in the darkness of deceit is to hate the light of truth. Jesus said, "This is the verdict: Light has come into the world, but men loved darkness instead of light because their deeds were evil. Everyone who does evil hates the light, and will not come into the light for fear that his deeds will be exposed" (John 3:19–20).

Once the Devil's language becomes established in a person, the appetite for it grows. The trap is set, and the victim becomes hopelessly entangled in the web of lies he has created. A spider can walk around on her web without getting stuck in it, but the liar can't.

One reason for this is "the Rule." We can disobey God, but we cannot outsmart Him. He has hard wired some mechanisms in place within us that bring about painful consequences for lying. These consequences take us by surprise when we violate the Rule. It is a corollary of the Golden Rule and goes like this, *what you do to others you will do to yourself,* whether you are aware of it taking place or not. Jesus did not bother to explain why it is so good to obey the Golden Rule; He just expected us to obey it. If we obeyed it we would never have to experience the negative consequences of the Rule.

When the Rule is applied to lying it goes like this, *if you lie to others you will lie to yourself.* It is a hardware problem that the liar cannot repair with the most sophisticated software. People without a love of the truth will ultimately be caught by the Rule. Scripture repeatedly tells us to watch our words carefully, but the warnings fall on deaf ears.

Since the liar has chosen the Devil's native language as his own, certain consequences follow. The most damaging consequence is that the liar believes his own lies. Once he believes his own lies, his ship has been torpedoed. There is no longer any way to obtain true, reliable, and accurate information about himself from himself. Until the Truth sets him free he will be stumbling, bumbling, and wandering in a desert of his own deceit.

Let me illustrate this with an example from my counseling experience. I worked with a man I'll call Larry that got caught in this trap. I met Larry in counseling years ago, and I thank him for all he taught me in spite of the fact that he almost drove me crazy. Larry believed his own lies. He told his wife Sally and me that he would never hit her again. But there was a problem. Larry told Sally that several times before I met them. Sally knew that Larry's words were meaningless, but Larry never figured it out. If he knew, he never acknowledged it to us. He wrote a love poem to Sally and asked to read it to her in session. He was convinced that this nice gesture would smooth out any ruffled feathers from the most recent violent episode. Sally was completely unmoved by his efforts. In fact, the words seemed to irritate her as he read them. Larry was bewildered by the fact that his wife no longer believed his words. Why? Because Larry still believed them. He believed his own lies, and he expected his wife to also believe them. That's what lies did to Larry.

"What's wrong with her?" he demanded. Larry should have asked, "What's wrong with me?" How was Sally to know who he really was and what he really meant when he spoke to her? His words were so confusing for her. He told her that he hated her when he was hitting her, and he told her that he loved her when he wanted to make up. "Can both fresh water and salt water flow from the same spring?" (James 3:11). No, they can't. Larry tenaciously clung to the hope that his empty words carried meaning without any evidence to prove it. He was deceived, like so many, and by his own lies. He lied to his wife, he lied to me, and he lied to himself. Lying became his language. Larry had grown so accustomed to lying that my efforts to tell him the truth sounded like Hebrew, Yiddish, and Farsi. Liars, once enslaved by their own lies, cannot understand and embrace the truth. It simply makes no sense to them any more.

People who lie to others also lie to themselves. They cannot help it. You may ask "who in their right mind would lie to themselves?" Anybody that tells herself she will cut back on the pie this Christmas and doesn't. The man with a drinking problem that tells himself that one drink really won't hurt anything. The unhappily married woman that tells herself "Jesus would want me to be happy" prior to seducing another woman's husband. The teenage boy who tells himself that Jesus is the Lord of his life on Sunday and acts like the Devil is during the rest of the week. The list is endless.

That is the problem with lying. We end up lying to ourselves. That's only fair, isn't it? If I choose to lie to you, I end up lying to myself too. If the reliability of my words is unimportant when I say them to you, they will become equally unimportant (meaningless) when I say them to me. I end up treating myself the same way I treat others. If lying is my language, how could I understand or speak anything else? What if lies were allowed to sneak into your language? Could you tease it out? Could you resist the temptation to believe your own lies as they were repeated throughout the day? Or, would they slither past your conscious mind unnoticed? The question is rhetorical. They *will* slither past your conscious mind unnoticed.

Even the Devil can't outsmart the Rule. Have you ever wondered, "Why does the Devil continue to pile additional judgment on himself? If he is so smart, why doesn't he just stop the evil right now?" Jesus gives us some insight into that question when He says, "there is no truth in him" (John 8:44). He cannot accept the truth about himself, his plans, and his destiny. The Devil is utterly enslaved by his own lies. He still believes that evil will triumph over good. Why? Because he has lost touch with the truth.

Like a hopeless addict he still believes he's in control of the situation. The truth is what sets us free, but according to Jesus the truth is not in him. What a pitiful situation. Great intelligence, energy, and power, but he is completely twisted and enslaved by his own lies and pride. Have you noticed that some people are like that too?

This is most obvious in addiction. Lying produces a number of problems and traps. None are more difficult to deal with than addiction. I was at a professional conference on addiction many years ago in which the speaker said, "All addicts are liars." The statement struck me sideways at first. "How does this guy know that? Isn't that a harsh, dogmatic thing to say about such a diverse group of people?" Yet, as I considered his statement in the days that followed, what he was saying began to make more sense. After all, when I was caught in an addictive trap, I lied to myself repeatedly for years without a clue that I was hopelessly trapped. I foolishly believed that my empty promises to myself to change would one day magically take effect and free me. Promise after promise to change and improve went unheeded, just more empty lies.

Addiction and lying are soul mates. Where you find one, you'll find the other every time. In fact, they are so closely linked that it is hard to determine which one comes first. Does the liar become addicted because his words of self-restraint are worthless? Or, does the addicted individual start to lie to himself and others to cover the shame of his inability to control himself? Both absolutely occur, but I believe that the lie is the initiating factor for a couple of reasons. The first is the abundance of scripture like this one in the Proverbs: "A man of perverse heart does not prosper; he whose tongue is deceitful falls into trouble" (Prov. 17:20). The deceitful tongue precedes falling into trouble. Lying ushers in addiction. Paul uses the same sequence in the New Testament: ". . . while evil men and impostors will go from bad to worse, deceiving and being deceived" (II Tim 3:13).

The second reason is based on God's intense hatred for lying and the numerous warnings He gives us to avoid it in scripture. "There are six things the Lord hates, seven that are detestable to him: haughty eyes, a lying tongue, hands that shed innocent blood," (Prov. 6:16–17). Only pride is listed above lying on the list of things the Lord hates. Lying even tops killing innocent people on the list. Maybe it's worse than we suspected. Maybe we should stop lying, even the little white ones.

Lies will take over your life if you embrace them on any level. It is a scary thought, but lies have a life of their own, *an energy of their own,* that leads to death. You cannot embrace them without getting burned. They have a way of taking over. They spread like wild fire. "Consider what a great forest is set on fire by a small spark. The tongue also is a fire, a world of evil among the parts of the body. It corrupts the whole person, sets the whole course of his life on fire, and is itself set on fire by hell" (James 3:5–6).

Why do people love darkness and lies when it

would be so much better to live in light and truth? The answer is found in their master. Your master takes you in the direction he's going, but his pull is so subtle that you think you are in charge. We are slowly being conformed to the image of our master, either increasingly truthful or increasingly deceitful. "No one can serve two masters. Either he will hate the one and love the other, or he will be devoted to the one and despise the other" (Matt. 6:24). Which way is your master taking you?

When Christ is our master, His words will actually create and sustain life. True and meaningful words cleanse, heal, and strengthen us. We cannot see the results immediately, but when we consistently circulate true, honest, just, pure, and lovely words through our hearts and minds, as Paul instructs us in Philippians 4:8, they cleanse us. Jesus said it like this "Sanctify them by the truth; your word is truth" (John 17:17). God's truthful words actually cleanse us in some inscrutable way. Words, like life-giving blood, are continually circulating through the chambers of our spiritual heart. *The truth will invigorate our innermost being, and lies will suck the life out of it.*

Chapter 4
Empty Words
(Symptom #2)

The more the words, the less the meaning, and how does that profit anyone?

—Ecclesiastes 6:11

The following interaction took place in the lobby of a mental health center I worked at years ago. It involved a grandmother and her wiggly young grandson who I'll call Junior. Grandma, Junior and everyone in earshot of their struggle was eager for Mom's appointment to come to an end. The interaction went something like this: "Come over here and sit down . . . I said get over here right now . . . I mean it . . . One, Two, Three . . . Did you hear me? . . . You'd better get over here right now young man . . . I'm going to wear you out . . . Come here . . . When your Momma comes back you're gonna get it . . . Come here I said."

The interaction continued much longer and

became louder and more vile than I want to record here, but you get the drift. Grandma never realized that her words meant nothing to her grandson. She could have been whistling "Dixie" with similar results and a lot less aggravation. That poor woman and everyone in the lobby that day was happy to see Junior's mother return from her counseling session.

Junior knew something about Grandma that she had not figured out yet. Grandma's words made the same sounds as real words, but they did not have any meaning attached. At the ripe old age of seven he had her figured out. He knew that her words–her commands as well as her threats–were empty, absolutely meaningless. She had no intention of backing them up with action.

Years ago, I wasn't doing much better than Grandma. The difference hinged on who we were trying to control. My empty words could not control the heathen on the inside (my flesh). Grandma's empty words were unable to control the little heathen on the outside (Junior). Neither heathen was listening, but we both kept talking in hopes that change would magically occur. Neither of us realized that empty words cannot change anything, no matter how many are used or how loud they become.

Solomon had Grandma in mind when he penned these words: "The more the words, the less the meaning" (Eccles. 6:11). The interaction between Grandma and Junior is an illustration of what I mean by the term "empty words." They are words that carry little, or in Grandma's case, no meaning at all.

Empty Words *(Symptom #2)*

They make sounds like real words, but they produce no action. They can be completely ignored without consequence. These words are literally nothing but hot air. Like lying, empty words are a symptom of an infection of Meaninglessness. Sometimes they are used as threats, like Grandma used them. But sometimes they are used in the form of promises.

I met a couple I'll call Steve and Jan very early in my counseling career at a center dealing primarily with family violence. Steve appeared to be a really nice guy. He was clean cut and well mannered. Jan didn't say much and didn't seem to want to be in my office. Steve taught me some important lessons about family violence and played a significant role in waking me up to the problem of Meaninglessness. Our first session took place soon after the couple's most recent violent episode. Steve cried a lot and begged Jan not to leave him during that session. At one point he got down on his knees, looked into Jan's eyes and said "I promise baby, it will never happen again." It sounded good to me. There were tears, emotion, and promises to change. I was proud of the role I played in facilitating such a life-changing session. They rescheduled but didn't keep the appointment.

About six months later they were back in my office after more physical abuse. The session was a replay of our first session with one exception. This time, after his promise that it would never happen again, I said "Steve, you promised Jan that the last time I saw you." He said, "This is different. I really, really mean it this time." He had me fooled. I thought that he really meant it in the first session. Again, the couple rescheduled but didn't keep the appointment.

About six months later they were back in my office again after more violence, and the third and final session looked just like the first two, with one exception. This time, after his promise to never hit her again, I said "Steve, how can you expect Jan to believe you? Your words don't mean anything, do they?" He seemed shocked that I could question his emotional, tear-stained words. After all, he believed them without any evidence that they were true, and he expected the same from me.

That's the problem with empty words and lies. The issuer becomes convinced that they are true without any evidence to support it. Once this occurs, the steel door clangs shut, and the prisoner enters a cage that only God can free him from. Empty words are like lies in that they render verbal communication unreliable, untrustworthy, and meaningless. Like lies they cause us to pay less and less attention to the speaker. They disconnect the speaker from his relationships with God and men. Who in their right mind would pay attention to the words of a liar or someone using empty words? Both lies and empty words train the listener to ignore a person's words, which is dangerously close to ignoring the person behind those words. It's fair to say, that in a sense, they take the life of the speaker. Lies and empty words take their credibility, their reputation (their "name"), their relationships, and their freedom. What else is left?

Empty words and lies took the freedom of

many of the men I met in a small county jail where I taught a Bible study. Many of the inmates from our Bible study could get out of jail, but they couldn't stay out. They would confidently assure me that we would never see each other in jail again, but in too many cases, things didn't work out that way. The words that represented their strongest desire–staying out of the county jail–were so riddled with holes by Meaninglessness that they were incapable of carrying any meaning. What a helpless feeling, making promise after promise and then watching your best intentions fade like the mist on a summer morning. These men were prisoners, not only of the county jail, but to their meaningless words that had lost the power to direct their course through life. Many went through life like a tumbleweed: no brakes, no steering wheel, and no map, waiting for the wind from the next fire to draw them into it.

Most of the prisoners I met were addicted to something, be it alcohol, drugs, violence, or some sort of excitement. Addiction represents the extreme end of the continuum of empty words. If you have struggled with addiction or know someone who has, you know that words are empty for the addict. They may swear, "This will be the last time . . . I'll pay you back," etc., but sadly, their words are seldom reliable. This is especially true when the words relate to the addiction itself. For example, an alcoholic may get to work on time and put in an honest day's work, but it's anybody's guess when asked, "Did you stop at the liquor store on the way home?"

Addicted individuals believe, despite overwhelming evidence to the contrary, that their empty words are true. When they say they don't have a problem, they actually believe it. They are the most vulnerable to believing their own empty words. That's a consequence of lying and using empty words. The user begins to believe them. Addicts, like all the rest of us, tend to believe what they tell themselves whether evidence supports it or not. Their mind is transformed over time to accept almost any falsehood and reject the truth. It's an amazing phenomenon.

The scary part about this phenomenon is that it is not isolated to addicts and inmates. It has crept unnoticed into our sanctuaries. The problem has gotten out of hand. We are ignoring the covenants that we have made with the Lord Jesus Christ and with our mates. "Jesus is my Lord" and "Till death do we part" are starting to ring hollow. Even our most sacred words are becoming increasingly ignored, empty, and meaningless. And this paves the way for the next symptom.

Chapter 5
Damaged Relationships
(Symptom #3)

There is a weird power in a spoken word . . . And a word carries far–very far–deals destruction through time as the bullets go flying through space.

—Joseph Conrad

Frank's father told him to jump. "I'll catch you," he said, "just trust me." He looked up at Frank with open arms. At his father's insistence, Frank summoned all the courage he could muster and jumped to his father's outstretched arms. Tragically, his father stepped away and Frank hit the ground with a thud, followed by a whimper. His father said "Let that be a lesson to you. Don't ever trust anyone." Frank learned the lesson well. He never trusted his father or anyone else, and that decision left him lonely, depressed, and miserable. He came in for counseling in an attempt to find out why he couldn't sustain a relationship with a woman, or with anyone else for that matter.

We instinctively recoil at the thought of such betrayal. "How could he do that to his own son?," we ask. But without being aware of it, we could be teaching our children similar messages about trust on more subtle levels. We could teach our children, family, and friends to disregard our words and never realize that we were doing it if Meaninglessness gets a foothold in our life.

Relational damage always accompanies an infection of Meaninglessness. Relationships are built on trust. They require trust like our body requires food and water, or they will die. Trust is built by reliable, meaningful words. For example, if I tell you that I'll pick you up at 5:00 a.m. and show up at 6:30 a.m. without a valid excuse, trust will be damaged. If I have an appointment with my doctor at 2:00 p.m., and he sees me at 3:45 p.m., trust will suffer. If I tell my daughter she is grounded for two weeks and ignore the restrictions when my angry mood subsides, trust is damaged. On the surface everything looks fine. I'm happy that I don't have to deal with the grief of monitoring all the rules. She's thrilled that she can use the phone again to talk to her friends. But she is left wondering if I really mean what I say, if my words really carry any weight. As a result of her uncertainty, she'll send me more tests to see how reliable I am.

This process of uncertainty and testing strains the fabric of any relationship and could be avoided if we looked at our words like God looks at them. Words are nothing but combinations of sounds. They make recognizable noises that dissipate quickly after they are spoken. But they form the foundation that supports our relational life, and to take them lightly is to take the relationship lightly.

Tracy was a woman who took words lightly for years before coming in for counseling. She was very depressed and completely frustrated with her teenage son. She and her son, who I'll refer to as Bobby, played a little game after school on a regular basis. This is how the game went:

Bobby comes home from school, lies down on the couch and turns on the TV.
> **Mom**: "You need to do your homework."
> **Bobby**: "I will."

Nothing happens for fifteen minutes.
> **Mom**: "I told you that you need to do your homework."
> **Bobby**: "I will when this show is over."

Mom comes back after the show is over, and Bobby is still watching TV.
> **Mom**: "I thought I told you to do your homework."
> **Bobby**: (*in an irritable voice*) "Okay, Okay."

Mom waits fifteen minutes and finds Bobby still watching TV. Now she's really mad.
> **Mom**: "Turn the TV off, now!"

Bobby pouts and goes to his room. Mom feels angry, frustrated and guilty about losing her temper.

This frustrating game, or one like it, goes on

almost every day in many homes. Nobody would ever say "Hey, that was fun, let's play this again sometime," but many families play it over and over because they are caught in the bondage of Meaninglessness. They are caught because they do not understand the need to pay close attention to their words. Finding the way out requires thinking outside of the box. Thinking outside the box, for most of us, means placing the highest value on our words. The solution is elusive if we have become accustomed to ignoring our words.

The heart of the problem is a growing disrespect for and mistrust of each other's words. For example, if Mom means "turn the TV off and do your homework," she will stay and ensure that it is done. If Bobby means "I'll turn it off after the show is over," he will turn the TV off. But Mom and Bobby don't really mean what they say. They play games with meaningless words until Mom gets angry. Mom and Bobby are training each other to ignore words, their own and each other's. The initial string of words in their daily dialogue has no effect on the other person. Those words are, for all intents and purposes, meaningless. This communication process breeds disrespect for both Bobby and Mom and dismantles trust within their relationship.

People are prone to believe that their words have meaning even when all the evidence suggests otherwise. It's a fascinating blind spot that we humans have, and Satan takes full advantage of it. Rather than paying close attention to our words, as the Bible teaches, most of us simply turn up the volume and emotional intensity of our words for a "quick fix," which only causes more problems. Mom never suspects that her problem with Bobby is related to the lack of attention both she and Bobby pay to her words. The use of meaningless words forms a blind spot over time. That's why she came to counseling. She couldn't see how to get out of the frustrating mess she was caught in.

More could be said about children and parenting, but many problems could be avoided and repaired by watching our words like a hawk and doing everything we say we will do, when we say we will do it. The more inconvenient it is to honor our words, the better. When our children see our determination to do what we say we will do, or die trying, they will listen to what we say. However, if we ignore our words, we will teach them to also ignore our words—and worse—their words.

I wonder what would happen to the profession of psychotherapy if we paid close attention to the words of Solomon "He who guards his mouth and his tongue keeps himself from calamity" (Prov. 21:23). This is great medicine for the heart of a child and far less expensive than therapy.

The damage to trust occurs due to unreliable, meaningless words. Trust is built by dependable words, and relationships are built on trust. Consequently, words form the foundational layer of relationships. They are far more important than a modern, non-Biblical mind-set could ever imagine, and they must be guarded like valuable treasure if we want to have the kind of relationships that people dream about having—honest, devoted, sincere, self-sacrificing, and lasting. The parent-child relationships discussed demonstrate the same principles present in all relationships. Truly satisfying relationships, with our children as well as others, are built on the foundation of trustworthy, meaningful words.

David found his relationship with King Saul to be far short of satisfying. The story of David and King Saul in I Samuel, chapters 18–26 illustrates two extreme positions in the way men view their words and in the way God views these men. It's hard to think of a Biblical character who uses words more flippantly than King Saul. His words are frequently absolutely meaningless chatter. But none guard their words more diligently than David.

David made a covenant with Jonathan, King Saul's son, that he chose to honor at an enormous cost. The covenant stipulated that David would show Jonathan "unfailing kindness" and that he would extend this kindness to the rest of his family. Jonathan could see the handwriting on the wall. David was going to be the king one day, and that meant that Jonathan and his descendants would most likely be exterminated in the process.

The years that followed were not good to Saul and his descendants. They lost their fortunes and most of them lost their lives through a series of unfortunate circumstances not at all related to David. Later, when David's kingdom was firmly established, he said, "Is there anyone still left of the house of Saul to whom I can show kindness for Jonathan's sake?" (II Sam. 9:1). Only one of Jonathan's sons remained. He was a crippled man named Mephibosheth. David commanded that everything that belonged to Saul and his family be given to Mephibosheth. Let me assure you, those holdings were significant, even to a wealthy king like David.

By today's worldly standards, David was insane. He didn't have to give Mephibosheth anything. In fact, he was expected, by the standards of the day, to put him to death. But he chose to give him vast resources of land and wealth. What was it about David that made him such a good friend? David's words were as good as gold. *And it is those kinds of words that build friendships people today can only dream about.*

In stark contrast, Saul's words meant nothing. Even his most sacred words were absolutely worthless. Jonathan once begged Saul not to kill David. "Saul listened to Jonathan and took this oath: 'As surely as the Lord lives, David will not be put to death'" (I Sam. 19:6). This solemn oath, invoking the name of the Lord, only endured for four verses. Verse 10 records Saul trying to "pin him [David] to the wall with his spear" (I Sam. 19:10).

In spite of the murderous efforts by Saul, twice David generously spared his life. Each time, Saul offered shallow words of repentance before trying to murder him again. Although a king, Saul's words reflected a spiritual pauper. They were meaningless.

Notice the way David viewed words. He valued the man and described him as righteous who *"keeps his oath even when it hurts"* (Psalm15:4). Yes, David placed great value on his words, and he became the father, as well as the instructor, of Solomon, the wisest man who ever lived. He knew the value of words, and he knew the value of trust.

Trust is breaking down today. It's breaking down in marriage, family, church, business, and government. This fact should come as no surprise. Words are used so lightly, so flippantly, today. The world conspires with the flesh and the Devil to subtly remove the meaning from words, hence, from relationships. When words of agreement failed, a handshake was required. When a handshake failed, a contract was needed. When a contract failed, the number of lawyers tripled in a thirty-year period to deal with all the chaos. Please tell me, where do we go from here?

Chapter 6
Self-control Problems
(Symptom #4)

If anyone is never at fault in what he says, he is a perfect man, able to keep his whole body in check. When we put bits into the mouths of horses to make them obey us, we can turn the whole animal.
—James 3:2–3

People bring their problems to counselors. Self-control problems up to and including addiction are some of the most difficult and baffling symptoms of Meaninglessness. Faddish approaches in psychotherapy have promised hope but seldom deliver. Years ago, one of those new approaches involved sticking something like an ice pick through the eye socket into the frontal lobe of the brain and scrambling it like an egg. The procedure was called a frontal lobotomy, and it seemed to help people calm down a lot, but there was an unpleasant side effect–a blank stare. Thankfully, that fad has passed away.

Some counselors still hypnotize their clients;

some do age regression or rebirthing; some still encourage primal screams. Some see almost every problem as the result of sexual abuse, and they search diligently for these repressed memories. Too often they create them instead of finding them. And then there are some who search for the answers to self-control problems in a timeless book called the Bible.

The Bible verses above shed heavenly light on the problem of self-control. The words in those verses jumped off the page at me years ago. James makes it clear that some connection exists between our mouth and self-control. That fascinates me more than I can tell you. It's like a sign saying, *"GOLD BELOW . . . DIG HERE."*

How can a person's mouth affect the control of their body? I don't think it has anything to do with the teeth, tongue, or anything in the mouth. The context is not about food, so it's not about what you put in your mouth. The verses tie the mouth to the concept of self-control because of what comes out of the mouth–words.

Those little noises that we've learned to pay so little attention to just happen to be a priority in God's economy. If you doubt that, read through Psalms, Proverbs, Ecclesiastes and the book of James. Look for the references to how we use our words, tongue, and mouth; they are everywhere. That's how God lets us know that something is important to Him; He repeats it. And anyone who chooses to ignore God's priorities–*words*–can be identified by the loss of self-control. People are free to ignore God's priorities, but they are not free to enjoy it for long. The loss of self-control is a price we pay for ignoring our words.

I paid the price for years. The choice to take God's words of counsel and instruction so flippantly caused me to treat my own words of counsel and instruction the same way. That's only fair isn't it? If I ignore the instructions of the Creator of the universe, it's only fair that I would ignore my own. That's how God has hard wired the mind of man. If we ignore Him we are forced, without our awareness of the process, to ignore ourselves.

For example, if Bill flies to Las Vegas to gamble after telling himself and his wife that he will never go again, he is ignoring his own commands, instructions, and promises to himself and others. He is ignoring his words. If I were a gambler like Bill, I'd bet the farm that Bill is ignoring many of God's words of instruction, not only the ones warning us not to prosper at the expense of others (gambling). I know this because Bill cannot obey himself. It all started when he chose not to obey God. This is God's way of reminding us to take Him and what He says seriously. Those who refuse will become the slave of a self-control problem with no words to tame it.

Ignoring God's words and instructions made me unable to obey my own. I know that sounds strange, but that is exactly what takes place with self-control problems. In fact that's not a bad definition of a self-control problem. You can't get yourself to do what you tell yourself to do. It's like a rebellion from within where you ignore your own words of restraint. The flesh (the rebel within) is not obligated to take your words of restraint seriously if you don't. Therein is the link of self-control problems and Meaninglessness. Our words of self-restraint become meaningless when we are afflicted with Meaninglessness.

That's a lot of theory. Let's look at a practical example. Next Thanksgiving or Christmas you will probably be exposed to an incredible spread of fine desserts. If you are on a diet, your self-control will be tested. If you tell yourself, "Only one piece of Grandma's pecan pie this Christmas" and your words mean something, you'll keep the commitment. However, if your words are plagued with Meaninglessness, you'll end up in Grandma's pecan pie, ice cream, and the divinity that she makes just for you at Christmas. Meaningless, empty words cannot protect you from your fleshly lust. Pithy jingles like "A moment on the lips but a lifetime on the hips" are no help. Why? The pithy jingles don't mean anything either. When a person allows any of their words to go unheeded, all their words can go unheeded, especially words of self-control.

For some people it's a little more serious than pecan pie at Grandma's house. I met a young woman years ago who I'll call "Valerie." She came in to talk about a relational problem with her husband. Valerie gained a great deal of weight after getting married, and her husband was repulsed by it. The couple was struggling to survive financially, and he was infuriated by an expensive little habit that she had. Valerie drank a twelve-pack of Coke every day. To make matters worse, she was having some serious problems in controlling her diabetes. Unfortunately, she didn't like sugar-free Cokes and insisted on the ones with sugar. Her agreements with me to cut back in an effort to save her life and her marriage were just like the ones she made with her husband and herself. They were meaningless. *Valerie, like anybody who chooses to ignore their words of commitment, was like a tumbleweed near a forest fire.* They don't come equipped with brakes, and the wind is blowing in the wrong direction.

Controlling ourselves is one of the most difficult challenges in life. Most people give up and try to control someone else; it's so much easier. Many seek help from secular counselors for these problems. Some of them will help you fish the murky waters of the subconscious mind for the solution to your self-control problems. But before turning to them for help, I urge you to take a razor-sharp assessment of how you view words—both God's and your own.

Chapter 7
Inability to Connect with God
(Symptom #5)

But your iniquities have separated you from your God; your sins have hidden his face from you, so that he will not hear.

—Isaiah 59:2

I worked as a counselor in our county's Mental Health facility for several years. The arrival of the Sheriff's deputies always signaled trouble. They brought in people from the jail or the community, frequently in handcuffs, who needed to be assessed for a commitment hearing. The county judge almost always took our recommendation about whether to commit or release the individual.

My job was to determine if an individual was a threat to themselves or others. The stakes were high. If I determined that they were dangerous to others or that they could not care for themselves, psychiatric hospitalization almost always resulted. Few were happy with me or eager to go to our state hospital if that was my determination. Nobody ever came back from the hospital to say, "Thanks so much for sending me . . . It was a great experience . . . My, you did a good job." Sometimes it could get really ugly, and I dreaded making those tough decisions.

Sometimes the decision making process was brutal and deeply troubling. At other times, it was easy. The way people used their words helped me make the decisions. People who were disconnected from reality used words that reflected this fact. Their words made no sense, merely disconnected babbling in some cases. Sanity is measured, to a great extent, by how people use words. The more an individual uses meaningless words, the more insane they are.

For example, some people tried to convince me that they were Jesus Christ. That is quite literally nonsense; it's meaningless talk. Jesus will not allow anybody to handcuff him when he returns, nor would He ask me for a smoke break. I'm not going to listen to a man tell me that he is Jesus for long, and I don't think you would either, especially if you had others waiting on your services.

But I've wondered, does God listen when a man or woman spouts off meaningless nonsense? Or, does He tune out like I did? Does He pay close attention to the soul who issues promises and commitments to Him without substance, merely hot air? Is He satisfied by praise and petitions from those same lips? He knows if people truly mean what they say. But those making the promises often don't. People that use deceit with others, including God, use deceit on themselves without being aware of it. They believe their own lies. That's my greatest concern about the epidemic of Meaninglessness that I see ravaging our churches and our land. Why should God take us seriously?

The people that Malachi was talking about in the second chapter of his book fell into this trap. They thought that they could lie to God and still be taken seriously by Him. They didn't understand that God's choice to listen to their praises and petitions was based on their choice to keep their promises.

> Another thing you do: You flood the Lord's altar with tears. You weep and wail because he no longer pays attention to your offerings or accepts them with pleasure from your hands. You ask, 'Why?' It is because the Lord is acting as the witness between you and the wife of your youth, because you have broken faith with her, though she is your partner, the wife of your marriage covenant. (Mal. 2:13–14)

God's response to our offerings, praise, and petitions is tied to our response to our promises to Him and others. His response to us is linked to how we choose to look at our words of commitment to Him. If words of commitment go unheeded by us, then our words of petition and praise will go unheeded by God. That's only fair, isn't it? The level of integrity present in an individual's words is the most accurate reflection of their heart and spiritual life, not what they tell you or themselves about their heart and spiritual life.

James uses a spring of water to illustrate this point. "Out of the same mouth come praise and cursing. My brothers, this should not be. Can both fresh water and salt water flow from the same spring?" (James 3:10–11). *If we want God to take us seriously when we praise Him then we have to take our words seriously when we promise Him.* We cannot have it both ways. We can't say, "Listen to me when I praise you and beg you for help, but ignore me when I make sacred promises to you and others that I choose not to keep." Either our words mean something or they don't. Although many men and women are afflicted with the disease of Meaninglessness to varying degrees, God remains completely immune to it. The meaning of words is crystal clear to God. He employs no lawyers to help Him understand the meaning of our agreements with Him. People can mislead themselves and others with their words, but they cannot deceive God. If a man tells Jesus that he wants Him to be Lord and Savior, Jesus will know if he is really serious or not. It will be clear by the way he conducts his life. "The man who says 'I know him,' but does not do what he commands is a liar, and the truth is not in him" (I John 2:4).

The words of a young woman often come to mind as I consider these thoughts. My wife, Laura, was involved in a campus ministry at a local junior college years ago. Laura asked a young woman if she knew Jesus Christ as her Lord and Savior. The young woman replied "Oh yeah, I did that thing a long time ago." She put a check in her "get saved" box, but God alone knows if this young woman's soul belongs to Him or not. Her words did not reflect an ongoing hunger or thirst for righteousness. It sounded more like she checked something off a "to do" list years ago and then started doing her own thing.

My greatest concern, and a key motivation for writing this book, is that people surrounded by meaningless words tend to use those same meaningless words in their relationship with God. Many have duped themselves into a false sense of security by saying the words "Jesus is my Lord and Savior." Those words reflect a new life in some, but only meaningless noise in others.

Saying those words when Paul wrote Romans could easily cost a man his life. Nero considered himself to be a god and was infuriated by the insult that one of his subjects would consider a poor Jew named Jesus to be their Lord. Anyone acknowledging Jesus as Lord and Savior within the Roman Empire at that time was deadly serious about it. Saying those words publicly could cost you your life. Those words could get you free admission to the Circus Maximus and an exciting encounter with a hungry lion. Anyone saying the words "Jesus is Lord" would be deadly serious about them before allowing them to roll off of his tongue.

But now things are very different. For many,

those words have come to mean nothing at all. They have no observable impact on some lives. "If anyone considers himself religious and yet does not keep a tight rein on his tongue, he deceives himself and his religion is worthless" (James 1:26). People are capable of deceiving themselves. Meaninglessness has the power to render a man's religion "worthless" without him ever being made aware of it. That is the greatest danger of Meaninglessness.

Chapter 8
Broken Vows
(Symptom # 6)

Count it the greatest sin to prefer life to honor, and for the sake of living to lose what makes life worth having.

—Juvenal

When a man makes a vow to the Lord or takes an oath to obligate himself by a pledge, he must not break his word but must do everything he said.

—Numbers 30:2

Laura's uncle told me a story about a vow that radically changed his life. The effects of that vow live on today in the lives of his sons. Uncle Bill made the vow during World War II on a snowy day in January of 1945. The Battle of the Bulge was still raging, and his infantry unit, which was attached to the Army's 82nd Airborne Division, was right in the middle of it.

Uncle Bill's platoon was in a firefight with what

appeared to be a simple German infantry unit. The Americans were getting the best of the Germans until a German tank came out of hiding to Uncle Bill's far left. Now if that happened to American soldiers in combat today, it would be no problem. A missile from an Apache helicopter would impact the tank's turret not long after the call for help went out. But on an overcast day in 1945, no fighter aircraft would be coming to the rescue. When that tank rolled out onto the field of battle, it represented something very different than it would to an American soldier today. It meant almost certain death.

Outside of supernatural intervention, every American solder exposed along that fence row had one small shot at survival–a bazooka. A brave American tried to get through the barbed wire fence with the bazooka to disable the tank; he didn't make it. His lifeless body and the bazooka were left dangling on the fence as the snow fell.

The tank then fired on every American position along that fence row, starting at Uncle Bill's left and systematically killing down the fence row towards his position on the far right side of the American line. This is how Bill Dean put it in his book *I Am a Survivor*: "The next shell was mine, and I knew it . . . I prayed a very simple but sincere prayer. It went something like this, 'Jesus, if You will allow me to live, I vow to do anything You ever ask me to do'" (55). Obviously, God spared Uncle Bill that day. His vow was probably not that unusual for combat veterans, but his decision to keep it probably was.

Combat has a way of getting a man's attention like nothing else. Looking down the muzzle of a tank gun has a way of making a man willing to consider making some changes in the way he lives. Not many can say they have ever had to face something like that. Except for driving down Highway 49 on New Year's Eve, my chances of experiencing a violent and painful death are relatively remote in the peaceful little community where I live.

People don't talk much about vows anymore. Some confusion exists regarding vows within the church. Some say that we should never vow because Jesus said "Do not swear at all: either by heaven, for it is God's throne . . ." (Matt. 5:34). In this passage Jesus is telling believers not to swear by *things* in an effort to get men to believe you. Simply let your yes be yes and your no be no. Don't try to rev up the integrity in your words by swearing. When a person of integrity says yes, that ought to be enough.

Swearing in an effort to get someone to believe you, and making a special commitment to God (a vow), are two entirely different things. Swearing is condemned by Jesus but vows are not. The vow is a tool that men use to help them do what they would not do otherwise. The Hebrew word translated "vow" is *nadar. The Complete Word Study Old Testament* defines it like this: "to promise, vow. It is the act of verbally consecrating something to God."

David advises us in the Psalms to commit ourselves to the Lord with vows. "Make vows to the Lord your God and fulfill them" (Psalm 76:11). Vows are tools that can take us far beyond where our complacent flesh would like to drop us off. I don't know what Uncle Bill's life would have been like had that German tank not been there on that cold day in January of 1945, but my guess is that it wouldn't have been as rich as it has been. After the war, he became a pastor and had five sons, four of which are pastors today. I wonder how many lost souls have found Jesus because of that German tank and the vow that it evoked that day.

Before rushing into a vow to create a fulfilling life, it would be wise to read the rest of the story. The story on vows is not all roses, as the Bible attests and as I have personally experienced. Shortly before getting married I made a vow that changed my life too. I knew that the demands of marriage and family life would eliminate much of the free time that I used for spiritual disciplines like prayer, scripture memory, and Bible study. So I vowed that I would rise at a certain time every morning, six days out of the week, to invest in spiritual growth.

My vow was easy to make. The sun was going down on a beautiful day as I topped a hill with a scenic view on Highway 14. It just seemed like the right thing to do, until the next morning. What was I thinking? Immediately my flesh began to waffle, saying, "This is ridiculous . . . You're not going to get enough sleep . . . God wouldn't want you to go through with this silly vow . . . That was just foolish talk . . . He knows you meant well, but let's be real." My waffling sounded a lot like the waffling Solomon wrote of in Ecclesiastes.

> When you make a vow to God, do not delay in fulfilling it. He has no pleasure in fools; fulfill your vow. It is better not to vow than to make a vow and not fulfill it. Do not let your mouth lead you into sin. And do not protest to the temple messenger, 'My vow was a mistake.' Why should God be angry at what you say and destroy the work of your hands? (Eccles. 5:4–6)

    The battle was on; it was "Being reasonable and getting more sleep" versus "Doing what I vowed to God I would do." Sometimes being reasonable won, and I was miserable. Sometimes I kept my vow, and my flesh was miserable. This went on, I'm ashamed to say, for several years.

    Finally I said "Okay, let's settle it once and for all." I proposed a month long test in which I would wake up whenever I pleased just to see if the extra sleep might be the answer to the depression I was going through. It wasn't. I've never been so miserable in my life. I've kept the vow since then. But I've wondered, what would my life be like today without that vow? I don't know the answer to that question, but I do know this. Those early hours have been the best investment I have ever made, and I would not change them for the world.

    If I had continued to choose sleep over honoring my vow, I was heading for a spanking. According to Solomon, some pretty hefty negative consequences follow breaking a vow. The Amplified Bible says it like this "Why should God be [made] angry at your voice and destroy the work of your hand?" (Eccles. 5:6) Why did my voice make God angry when I was not honoring my vow? *Because if I attach no real value or honor to my solemn vow to God, what does that say about the more ordinary communications that I send Him, like praise? It says that the praise is to be taken just as seriously as the promise.* That's the rub.

Promises, vows, and covenants (we'll talk about them next) are as reliable as our words can be. When they crumble, what does that say about the rest of our words? When they are feeble, so is the likelihood of real trust and intimacy with anybody, including God. That's why words are so important, and that's why He's "made angry" when people break their vows to Him. Flaky promises equal flaky relationships, and that's not why He made us. He was looking for the kind of relationships that people dream about. But He stands ready to forgive when a Christian acknowledges broken vows for what they are–sin.

CHAPTER 9
Covenants

One of the words of Scripture that seems to have gone out of fashion is the word "covenant." There was a time when it was the keynote of our theology and of the Christian life of strong and holy men.
—Andrew Murray

Allowing any of our words to ring hollow is a serious problem. But the price for allowing our words of covenant to ring hollow is devastating. Covenant is a concept that has eroded during recent times. In fact, over a hundred years ago it was eroding. In 1898 Andrew Murray wrote "One of the words of Scripture that seems to have gone out of fashion is the word 'covenant.' There was a time when it was the keynote of our theology and of the Christian life of strong and holy men" (*The Two Covenants,* 7). If the study of covenant was going out of fashion in 1898, it is safe to say that it is completely out of fashion today.

What is a covenant? The "Hebrew and Chaldee Dictionary" in *Strong's Exhaustive Concordance of the Bible* defines it as "a compact (because made by passing between pieces of flesh):–confederacy, covenant, league." In the purest sense of the word, it is two becoming one. Much more than a simple agreement, promise, or vow, it is a union.

Why do people make covenants? The covenant serves the dual purpose of guaranteeing and unifying. A covenant serves as the ultimate guarantee of loyalty that one party gives to the other. The covenant guarantees that both parties will do what they have agreed to do or die trying. It is quite literally a binding agreement which unifies or binds the parties together.

Sounds serious, doesn't it? It is. To enter covenant is to be, quite literally, deadly serious about an agreement. Some relationships are so important to maintain that they require this level of commitment. Hence, God established the binding agreement called covenant. He initiated one with a man He called his friend, Abram, in the fifteenth chapter of Genesis. God took on the form of a smoking firepot with a blazing torch as He passed between the pieces of the five animals sacrificed especially for this ceremony with Abram. As the smoking firepot with a blazing torch began to move, God was saying, "My promise to you is so reliable that I am willing to be treated just as these animals–hacked in two at the spine–if I break it." Who in his right mind would go into an agreement like this without the supreme intention of keeping it? The Precept Ministries International's *Covenant* study states:

Before or sometime during this 'walk into death' between the pieces of the sacrifice, there was the understanding that if the covenant were broken by either party, they were calling upon God to 'do so to me as has been done to this animal if I break this covenant.' In other words, 'If I fail to keep this covenant, may I die even as this animal has died.' Or, to put it even more succinctly, 'God, kill me if I break this covenant' (36).

The self-maledictory oath is one of the features of a covenant that sets it apart from a mere promise, a contract, or a vow. This oath means "let these bad things happen to me if I fail to keep this covenant." What bad things? As the covenanting partners gazed down at the pieces of slaughtered animals that they walked through while making the agreement, they were reminded of their own demise if they failed to honor the covenant. The self-maledictory oath invites God to kill the one who fails to keep the agreement.

Asking God to kill me if I break a covenant is a frightening thought. How many today embrace this awareness when they say, "Till death do we part?" Would people try harder to get along if failing to get along led to certain death? I think so. Covenants were designed to produce the absolute assurance of lifetime loyalty between the covenanting parties. The seriousness of violating a covenant was designed to protect people from a fleshly tendency to seek what is off limits, to betray, to lie, and to cheat. Covenants ensured those depending on their partner's promise that they will do what they said they would do or die trying.

The covenant is an insurance policy taken out on the issuer's words. In the past, if the policy didn't pay, the insurer understood that God had been invited to take his life. *This was the clear understanding for centuries, but it began to change as integrity was pushed aside by convenience and honor was subdued by self-interest.* These changes have accelerated rapidly in the past sixty-five years to our detriment both personally and corporately.

Changes in the way we view our covenants have been greatly applauded by our flesh. These new flimsy agreements we call covenants are only a shadow of their predecessors. They are unable to keep our fleshly lusts from destroying us. We have forgotten why we need the powerful, yet cumbersome, constraints of covenant. It functions like a shark cage. Why would anyone stay within the restriction of a shark cage on the Great Barrier Reef when they could be swimming freely looking at all the pretty fish? Because Great White sharks are out there looking for some tasty tourists.

"Great Flesh" sharks, which swim around on the inside, are looking for some tasty marriages. They have big, dull, unfaithful eyes and sharp teeth that cut and tear at trust. Their noses are highly sensitive and draw them to things that are off limits. Like blood in the water, the forbidden draws these fleshly predators. They slide through the ocean depths of our soul, occasionally coming close to the surface to wreak havoc. They can shred a relationship just as quickly as a Great White Shark can devour a swimmer.

Our flesh is so dangerous that it needs the power of a self-maledictory oath to restrict it. The intended meaning of a covenant and this oath has faded over time so as to be unrecognizable by the modern observer. But has it faded in the mind of God? This question needs careful consideration from anyone in a covenant with God or man. *If God's thinking, attitude, and position on covenants has not changed over time, as have men's, we are way out of sync with Him.*

He watches as people flippantly profess the covenant of Christ as Lord and then ignore Him. He watches believers jump in and out of their covenant marriages. He doesn't pout or thunder in disapproval. He has already said all He is going to say on the subject. Although God remains quiet, He is watching our disobedience foolishly trying to hide behind His grace.

His grace fully covers our sin and is free of charge. But His fellowship comes at a price that meaningless words cannot afford. Too many seek His forgiveness but seem disinterested in His friendship. Friendship with Jesus Christ comes at a price–obedience. As Jesus said, "You are my friends if you do what I command" (John 15:14). We have forgotten that we are in covenant, the most intimate relationship possible, with Christ.

Chapter 10
Our Covenant with Christ

For this is My blood of the new covenant, which [ratifies the agreement and] is being poured out for many for the forgiveness of sins.
—Jesus (Matthew 26:28, TAB)

Every believer enters into a covenant with Christ whether they are aware of it or not. The New Testament tells the story of a new covenant, a new way of approaching and relating to a holy God. In this new covenant, Christians enter into a relationship with God under a new guideline, that of grace. This new covenant of grace changes everything. Jeremiah's prophesy of the changes that were to come is one of the most important announcements of the Old Testament. "'The time is coming,' declares the Lord, 'when I will make a new covenant with the house of Israel and with the house of Judah. It will not be like the covenant I made with their forefathers . . . '" (Jer. 31:31–32). The announcement of a new covenant was a complete mystery in the days of Jeremiah. The dynamics of its fulfillment remain mysterious even to this day.

The mystery of the new covenant with Christ is wrapped around a question. How does the believer become unified with Christ? Discussions about the Trinity are similarly baffling to the rational mind, which can only apprehend the concept but never fully comprehend it. How three persons are perfectly unified in one essence is beyond the rational power of the mind to fully comprehend. But they are. The mystery of this covenant with Christ is that two become united in such a way that the believer is described as being "in Christ," and Christ is described as being "in you." "[T]he mystery that has been kept hidden for ages and generations, but is now disclosed to the saints. To them God has chosen to make known among the Gentiles the glorious riches of this mystery, *which is Christ in you*, the hope of glory" (Col 1:26–27, emphasis mine).

This mystery cannot be perceived with the five senses, but it is no less real. In fact, it is more real, not less, than the senses can detect. The senses are not always trustworthy. But God's word is trustworthy, and His word says that when an individual places their trust in Christ, they become spiritually unified with Him. As Jesus said, "I pray also for those who will believe in me through their message, that all of them may be one, Father, just as you are in me and I am in you. May they also be in us so that the world may believe that you have sent me" (John 17:20–21).

The mystery of this union with Christ affects every relationship for a Christian. For example, if Frank is one with Christ, and Mike is one with Christ, then Frank and Mike have also been united in Christ. That is why "whatever you did for one of the least of these brothers of mine, you did for me" (Matt. 25:40). Consequently, when another believer does something to help Frank or Mike, they do it for Jesus because Frank and Mike are in Christ.

This is why Christians rightly call each other brother and sister. If they are one with Christ, then His Father becomes their Father, and the Father's children become siblings even though they may have never met. As Jesus said, "On that day you will realize that I am in my Father, and you are in me, and I am in you" (John 14:20).

This explains Christ's frequent command to love one another. And, why our *un*willingness to love each other is literally such a heartrending thing to God. Although our hearts may have become hardened and insensitive to the division in the body of Christ, His has not. His standard is unity, for as He said, "I in them and you in me. May they be brought to complete unity to let the world know that you sent me and have loved them even as you have loved me" (John 17:23). Without this unity, the Christian's witness to a lost and dying world is severely compromised. Seriously considering the implications of our covenant with Christ would make a difference in the way Christians treat each other and our testimony to the world.

Another aspect of this mysterious union, this covenant with Christ, is that it is infallible. God promised us eternal life if we believe in His Son. Nothing about that promise is shaky or temporary. This is the promise of the new covenant: "For God so loved the world that he gave his one and only Son, that whoever believes in him shall not perish but have eternal life" (John 3:16).

God enables and empowers believers to keep this New Covenant. In *The Two Covenants*, Andrew Murray writes: "The Old Covenant proved the need and pointed out the path of holiness; the New inspires the love and gives the power for holiness" (106). God is the one keeping it. That is why Paul says, "For I am convinced that neither death nor life, neither angels nor demons, neither the present nor the future, nor any powers, neither height nor depth, nor anything else in all creation, will be able to separate us from the love of God that is in Christ Jesus our Lord" (Romans 8:38–39). God is doing the keeping. Otherwise, it could not be infallible. This is not a license to sin but rather the freedom to aim high, to completely surrender ourselves to Him.

True Christians can't escape it, nor would they want to. This is how John describes those who walked away from Christ after professing Him as Lord, "They went out from us, but they did not really belong to us. For if they had belonged to us, they would have remained with us; but their going showed that none of them belonged to us" (I John 2:19).

Those that belong to Christ in this new covenant have a symbol to remind them of their commitment. The Bible describes several covenants and the symbols that represent them. For Noah it was a rainbow. For Abraham it was circumcision and a name change. The symbol of the Old Covenant was the tablets of stone, the Law. But for the believer, it is communion, the celebration of two becoming one. As Jesus said, "This cup is the new covenant in my blood; do this, whenever you drink it, in remembrance of me" (I Cor. 11:25). Believers need to gaze on it frequently in order to remind themselves of who they belong to as they walk through the fleshly magnetism of the world.

The believer is joined to Christ in his spirit. This remains true whether he feels distant and discouraged or intimately connected to the Lord and eager to obey Him. Regardless of how the emotions ebb and flow, these words remain true: "But he who unites himself with the Lord is one with him in spirit" (I Cor. 6:17). This "one with him in spirit" is even more intimate than a marriage relationship in which two become "one flesh." Let's take a look at the marriage covenant and what "one flesh" means.

Chapter 11
The Marriage Covenant

By the power that Christ brought from heaven, mayst thou love me. As the sun follows its course, mayst thou follow me. As light to the eye, as bread to the hungry, as joy to the heart, May thy presence be with me, Oh one that I love, 'til death comes to part us asunder.
—Traditional Irish Wedding Vows

In addition to our covenant with Christ, most Christians will enter into a marriage covenant at some point in their life. Some aspects of the marriage covenant are similar to our covenant with Christ, and some are very different. Similarities include the fact that both of these covenants are not mere earthly agreements. They are both designed, ordained, and sanctioned by God. They are not of human origin. They also include God as either participant or witness. He is involved in both agreements, and He is very interested in their development and outcome.

Supernatural bonding takes place in both covenants which cannot be perceived with the five senses.

I remember taking a drive shortly after being married. My shiny new wedding ring indicated that I was married, but I didn't feel different at all. I walked the same way, talked the same way and still preferred ice cream to sorbet. No indication that my soul had been spiritually welded to my wife Laura's soul could be detected by my conscious mind. The senses cannot perceive the bond that God has put in place, but it is very real—not as tangible as the ring that represents it, but no less real.

Once established, both covenants remain in effect. Neither covenant can be altered. They may be ignored, violated, and broken, but they can never be altered. That's what makes covenants so good when they're good and so bad when they're bad. Entering into a covenant with another human being is a very risky proposition. It is a risk that few today are willing to fully embrace.

In the few states which currently offer covenant marriages, only three percent of the people choose the covenant option. Why? Because it's risky. If your dream marriage turns into a nightmare, you can't get out of it without paying a high price. What those 97% that opted out of a covenant marriage didn't know is that God considers them to be in one anyway. Marriage is a covenant relationship whether you check the "covenant" box on the form or not. They cannot be dissolved until their terms and conditions are fulfilled. Paul touches on this fact while explaining the new covenant of grace, "Brothers, let me take an example from everyday life. Just as no one can set aside or add to a human covenant that has been duly established, so it is in this case" (Gal. 3:15). Once "duly established" it cannot be set aside.

Just as with our covenant with Christ, the marriage covenant is a mystery. For two to become one is always a mystery when they appear to be so different, but that's what the Bible teaches, starting in Genesis and continuing throughout the New Testament. The Bible describes both of these unions as mysteries. They transcend our rational capacity to comprehend them.

The differences in the covenant with Christ and the marriage covenant are also important to note. Time of termination is a key difference. Marriage covenants terminate upon the death of either spouse, just as the agreement states: "Till death do we part." Some, only those happily married of course, think that they will continue to be married in heaven. They will, but to a different mate–Jesus. Unlike a marriage covenant, the believer's covenant with Christ never terminates. It will be transformed and consummated in some mysterious way after the marriage supper of the Lamb, but it will never terminate.

Another difference involves the nature of the connection. Covenanting spouses on earth become only "one flesh" with their husband or wife. "But he who unites himself with the Lord is one with him in spirit" (I Cor. 6:17). As the physical and the spiritual are of a different nature or essence, so are the covenants with man and with God.

The final difference noted involves the character of the spouse. Due to our human nature, marriages between humans are a dicey proposition. Humans fail each other, hurt each other, and in many cases, abandon their promises to each other. Marriage to a person like this can make the marriage covenant a shackle rather than a delight. The humanness of the marriage covenant gives it vulnerability, from a human perspective, that the covenant with Christ lacks. The song says, "Every day with Jesus is sweeter than the day before." Not every Christian can say that about their spouse.

Laura and I spent years together in which we couldn't say that about each other. This is probably a good time to share a little bit of our story with you. Meeting Laura was one of those rare occasions when God forcefully intervened in my life. I was thirty-three years old and unmarried. My hopes of finding a wife were growing bleaker with each passing year. I was a graduate student with no money, an old Volkswagen, and a hole in the bottom of my best pair of shoes.

One Sunday morning I was especially discouraged by my single status. As I trudged up the steps of a tiny church and then on to the creaky wooden floor of the sanctuary, I said to myself, "The teaching is excellent, but I'm never going to meet anybody here." A few moments later I was sitting on a pew near the front of the sanctuary, and these thoughts came to my mind: "Wait a minute, God is able to find a wife for me . . . In fact, He could bring the perfect woman to this church . . . In fact, He could bring her here today if He wanted to."

We rarely had visitors at that little church, but Laura was there that Sunday morning. She had come in quietly and was sitting a few rows behind me. I had no clue that my future wife was sitting behind me as I was reminding myself that God was still in charge. When my pastor asked her to introduce herself to the congregation, I turned around and couldn't believe my eyes. Not only had God found a wife for me, but He picked out a very lovely one. My pastor introduced us that day, and he married us a year later in that sanctuary.

That's when the trouble began. For several years I wondered if those encouraging thoughts in the sanctuary that day were really from God. As we got to know each other a little better, it became clear that we only had three things in common–we were both Christians, both stubborn (she likes the word "determined"), and we both preferred brown rice to white.

Laura's father was a football coach at a nearby junior college. "Coach" was six-three and probably about two-twenty-five. He led his team to a National Championship early in our marriage. Coach may have been anxious in some of those close games, but I never picked up on it from the stands. When he was a high school football coach, his assistants called him "Gunsmoke." Just like Marshal Dillon in the TV series, he never lost his cool and always seemed to be in control of the situation. He had many admirable qualities that I lack. Coach was the picture, etched in my wife's mind, of what a man should be. Coach was the epitome of the strong, silent type, even in death. Cancer took his life during our third year of marriage. The church was packed at his funeral, and many of his old players came back to honor him. He was a remarkable man, and I regret not getting to know him better.

Somehow Laura ended up with me. I'm a lot more like Ben Stiller than John Wayne. During difficult and tense situations I prefer to think and talk about them. Laura needs silence during those times. As you might suspect, we don't do so well during tense times. What invigorates me (sharing deep thoughts) fatigues her, and what feels good to her (silence), feels like rejection to me. The tension created by our different natural inclinations will be in our marriage until the day that we die. We deal with it much better than we used to, but when we choose to walk in our flesh, we still look and feel pretty much like 60-grit sandpaper to each other.

I remember a conversation we had years ago. We were sitting on the couch crying. Both of us preferred death to any more sanding down from each other. But we didn't see any options for an honorable escape from the prison that our marriage had become. I traveled a lot, and from time to time I secretly hoped that my plane would crash–pretty selfish, huh? By God's grace we held on to our covenant through those dark times.

In utter desperation we decided to pray about our marriage problems together. The prayers were brief at first, but as time passed we began to spend more time together in prayer. God's grace, our stubborn refusal to ignore our marriage covenant, and our prayer time together saved our marriage. Take away one of those three elements and who knows where we would be today.

The cross shows up in different places for different people. Some Christians have delightful marriages but experience the cross in other areas of life, like health, finances, or other relational issues. For Laura and me, our marriage has been our cross. We made a choice that felt like death (staying together), but it led to life. Like Jesus said "If anyone would come after me, he must deny himself and take up his cross daily and follow me. For whoever wants to save his life will lose it, but whoever loses his life for me will save it" (Luke 9:23, 24).

Laura and I chose the cross of staying together over the freedom from each other that our flesh craved. In the process, a little flesh died every day, while our spirits were being invigorated. I don't say this to brag or cause you embarrassment if your marriage has failed. If that's the case, my heart goes out to you. Instead, I say it to confront the lie that real peace is available in escaping one's cross. Running from your cross will only create distance between you and Jesus. "If anyone would come after me, he must deny himself and take up his cross daily and follow me" (Luke 9:23). It sounds like those who want to be close to Jesus won't be far from the cross He has selected for them.

In case you're wondering, I'm convinced that the encouraging thoughts that day in the sanctuary were from God. Laura has turned out to be the perfect wife for me. She's just exactly what I need, and I wouldn't trade Laura for the world.

Chapter 12
Why Christians Ignore Marriage Covenants

These divorce rates are a scalding indictment of what isn't being said behind the pulpit.
—Oklahoma Governor Frank Keating

People professing faith in Christ seem to be having a harder time staying married than non-believers in some parts of the country. In his article in *Christianity Today*, Ronald Sider notes "In many parts of the Bible Belt, the divorce rate was discovered to be 'roughly 50 percent above the national average.'" That is amazing isn't it? People that claim to possess God's love are unable to demonstrate that love in marriage any better than the "national average." Doesn't that strike you as a bit odd?

Several social factors contribute to high divorce rates. The feminist movement, the industrial economy, the removal of the social stigma of divorce, and the pervasive laziness that makes anything difficult appear to be wrong, all play a role in the demise of marriage. Christian and non-Christian marriages alike suffer because of these trends as well as from laws that don't support marriage, like no-fault divorce. Since its inception in 1969, divorce rates have climbed higher than the supporters of the law ever dreamed. Congressman Tim Penny of Minnesota, who voted for the law 30 years ago said, "I did not expect divorce rates would rise so dramatically. I did not foresee the approximately one million American children now affected annually by divorce, twice the number of 30 years ago" (quoted in the summer 1996 newsletter of the Center of the American Experiment).

Rather than discussing trends and laws that create social pressure on Christian marriage covenants, my focus here is on the spiritual problem. No Christian marriage covenant can be forced to submit to social trends or terrible legislation. Our problem is on the inside. Ignoring God's word, making meaningless marriage vows, and selfishly refusing to embrace the cross of a difficult marriage are spiritual problems.

Ignorance of God's word is slowly strangling the church. Would we ignore our covenants if we fully understood the gravity of the unions established? I don't think so. The study of covenant stood in the way of the freedom to divorce and remarry others in covenant relationships. It had to be muzzled to secure this freedom. Covenant is the glue that holds marriage together, but the flesh detests the confinement. The world, the flesh, and the Devil have been bucking and wiggling under the glue of covenant for centuries, and it's cracking.

Because of this cracked and tarnished image of what a covenant truly is, many believers marry with no idea of the spiritual responsibility they have shouldered during the marriage ceremony. The Christian marriage covenant has only one termination clause–death. Most Christians are not aware of this. Some don't want to know what God says because they fear they will become responsible to obey it once they know it. They do not understand that ignorance has never been an excuse for disobedience in the Bible. Consider this verse from Leviticus: "If a person sins and does what is forbidden in any of the Lord's commands, even though he does not know it, he is guilty and will be held responsible" (Lev. 5:17). Why? Because the Bible instructs us through repeated commands to "meditate on it day and night" (Josh. 1:8). The New Testament repeats the same refrain. "Do your best to present yourself to God as one approved, a workman who does not need to be ashamed and who correctly handles the word of truth" (II Tim. 2:15). Why would God reward ignorance of His word with innocence? That's a strange way to run an organization. That type of thinking doesn't work any better with God than is does with a state trooper. "I didn't know what the speed limit was back there." He'll say "The speed limit is clearly posted, sir. Where should we mail this citation?"

Governor Keating pointed his finger at pastors, and he was right to do so. But, it won't be my pastor who stands before God to give an account for my life one day. It will be me. I will be held accountable for my ignorance of God's word and the resulting disobedience. And I will lose the rewards, not my pastor.

Misuse, as well as ignorance of scripture, is another reason people break covenants. People that never crack their Bible open are quick to site the "exception clause" as a clean escape when marriage gets tough. Almost everyone seems to be aware of it, and almost everyone seeking a divorce is sure that their spouse has done whatever they shouldn't have done, but few can explain the exception clause when pressed. Godly men, who I appreciate and respect, differ on how to interpret these verses. With that said, I'd like to discuss the exception clause.

The exception clause is one of the more controversial texts in the Bible. It's difficult to interpret for a couple of reasons. First is the fact that Jewish customs surrounding engagement and marriage in the first century are very different than ours today. Secondly, the two verses in Matthew, written to a Jewish audience, do not appear to harmonize with the clear and consistent teachings on divorce and remarriage present in the books of Mark, Luke, Romans, and First Corinthians. Notice that I said they do not *appear* to harmonize with the other teachings. However, they are in perfect harmony with the other teachings of Jesus when viewed as they are intended to be viewed.

The confusion surrounding the exception

clause has created "wiggle room" for the flesh as it tries to free itself from the obligations present in a marriage covenant. The exception clause has become the leaky life boat for the flesh of Christians whose marriages are sinking in the icy waters of divorce. It holds out the false hope of rescue, but it is not seaworthy enough to cleanse the conscience of guilt. Many Christians are desperate to find a Biblical way out of a painful marriage, and the exception clause appears to offer a ray of hope in this dark sky, until you look at it closely.

This clause is mentioned twice in the Bible. Both occurrences are in the Gospel of Matthew, which was written to the Jews. The first is in the *Sermon on the Mount*, and the second is Matthew 19:9. This clause is not listed in Mark, Luke, Romans or First Corinthians, where the recipients were primarily gentiles and where the teachings on divorce and remarriage are clear and consistent.

What is different about the book of Matthew? And why does Jesus include this clause here but leave it out elsewhere? Matthew is unique among the gospels in that it was written to Jews. Jews had different customs. For example, when Joseph found out that Mary was pregnant, " . . . he had in mind to divorce her quietly" (Matt. 1:19). When is the last time you heard about an engaged couple in America getting a divorce? This was a Jewish custom. A divorce was required to terminate the covenant that Joseph had established with Mary in the pledging ceremony. In *Jewish Marriage Customs*, Dr. Renald Showers says,

"Once the bridegroom paid the purchase price, the marriage covenant was thereby established, and the young man and woman were regarded to be husband and wife" (2). Since the covenant had not yet been consummated in accordance with its stipulations, they were not "officially married" as we in America today look at being officially married. They were only "pledged" ("espoused" in the King James). This was the reason for the embarrassment about the pregnancy. If they had been married, like we look at being married today, the pregnancy would have been cause for celebration, not humiliation.

The two verses containing this clause in Matthew are almost identical. I chose Matthew 5:32 because of the clarity of the context in the surrounding passages. In this section of the *Sermon on the Mount* Jesus raises the standards, radically surpassing the teachings of the Law. It is now considered murderous to be angry with a brother (Matt. 5:22). Likewise, it is now viewed as adulterous to look at a woman lustfully (Matt. 5:28). The exception clause occurs right after Jesus tells his listeners to gouge out their eye and cut off their right hand if they cause them to sin (Matt. 5:29–30).

Nothing in the entire fifth chapter of Matthew leaves the reader with any sense that the old standards of thinking and behaving will remain in place. The chapter concludes with these words, "Be perfect, therefore, as your heavenly Father is perfect" (Matt. 5:48). Jesus introduces new standards that are impossible to conform to without the indwelling power of the Holy Spirit. This is the bar-raising context for the exception clause. The lofty standards for marriage that Jesus put in place in other New Testament passages are not lowered, as some suppose, in this passage. Nothing appealing to the flesh is offered up in this chapter. This is the wrong scriptural neighborhood for a gentile, searching for an escape from a miserable marriage, to be wandering through. It won't be found here.

So here is the verse that so many have said so much about, "But I say unto you, That whosoever shall put away his wife, saving for the cause of fornication, causeth her to commit adultery: and whosoever shall marry her that is divorced committeth adultery" (Matt. 5:32, KJV). Notice, I used the King James Version this time. Substituting the words "marital unfaithfulness" (NIV) for the word "fornication" (KJV) makes an already difficult verse virtually impossible to understand.

Jesus chose to use the word *porneia* in the exception clause. *The Complete Word Study Dictionary* defines *porneia* as "to commit fornication or any sexual sin." If Jesus meant to say adultery, or "marital unfaithfulness," as the NIV translates it, He would have chosen the word *moicheia,* which means "The act of adultery." It would have been the perfect word if that was what He meant to say. But fornication and marital unfaithfulness, just like *porneia* and *moicheia*, are different words that mean different things. Marital unfaithfulness is generally understood to be "adultery" not "fornication." Married people commit adultery, and unmarried teenagers commit fornication.

When we look at the exception clause in the fifth chapter of Matthew, we need to look at it like a Jew in the first century would look at it. The concepts of engagement, marriage, and divorce are communicated to us through a Jewish cultural lens in the first chapter with the story of Mary and Joseph, and the same lens should be used to observe the exception clause in the fifth chapter.

Joseph is described as Mary's husband in the first chapter. But the covenant that he established with Mary in the pledging ceremony had not been fulfilled and consummated as the agreement stipulated. He quietly considered divorcing her because he thought she had been unfaithful. Mary and Joseph had a marriage covenant in place, but it did not allow for sexual intercourse until the pledging period was completed, usually one year. That is not the way we do marriage today. Applying the exception clause to our marital customs only creates confusion.

Mary and Joseph are a perfect example of a couple who needed an exception clause. Here is a situation where one could be divorced for fornication and still be eligible for remarriage because the covenant had not yet been consummated by sexual intercourse. This is the heart of the confusion surrounding the exception clause. The couple is "married," and yet, from our modern perspective, they are not. When we marry in modern times, the covenant is almost always consummated on the same day. Little or no time is available for fornication with another partner to become an issue. Therefore, we don't need an exception clause which would allow for divorce in the event that our "spouse" was unfaithful during the pledging period, nor did we get one in the gospels of Mark and Luke, which were written to gentiles.

But a Jewish couple in the days of Jesus needed this exception clause. Their marital customs created the possibility that some hanky-panky might take place during the year-long pledging period. Jewish couples with these customs needed an exception clause, and they got one in the Gospel of Matthew. Jesus freed them to remarry if fornication took place in the pledging period but not if adultery took place after the marriage covenant was fully consummated.

In his article entitled "Did Jesus Say Adultery is Grounds for Divorce?" Jimmy Akin strongly argues that the answer is "no." He includes a quote worth pondering from John P. Meier's book *The Vision of Matthew*:

> [I]f Matthew were espousing adultery as grounds for divorce, he would soon run up against grave practical difficulties. In this hypothesis, Matthew would allow divorce and remarriage for a husband and wife who had committed adultery. But a husband and wife who remained faithful to each other would not be allowed to divorce; indeed their attempt at divorce would be considered adultery. Obviously, the only thing to do

for a faithful Christian couple who wanted a divorce would be to commit adultery, after which a dissolution of the marriage would be allowed. What we wind up with is divorce on demand, with a technical proviso of committing adultery. This all constitutes a strange church discipline, one in which adultery seems encouraged and fidelity discouraged (253).

That is the unspoken logic that lurks below the common understanding of the exception clause in the Evangelical Church today. The exception clause was never designed for gentiles, and it can never soothe the conscience of those who choose to break their marriage covenant. It will make no more sense to a gentile after the divorce than it does before the divorce. But the clear teachings from Mark, Luke, Romans, and First Corinthians will continue to nag the conscience of a Christian who has broken his covenant but who continues to read his Bible.

Look at this verse without the "except it be for fornication," inserted and observe. "But I say unto you, That whosoever shall put away his wife causeth her to commit adultery: and whosoever shall marry her that is divorced committeth adultery." It reads much like Luke 16:18: "Whosoever putteth away his wife, and marrieth another, committeth adultery: and whosoever marrieth her that is put away from her husband committeth adultery" (Luke 16:18, KJV).

The proper interpretation of this verse cannot

be made in a vacuum. It must be examined within the context in which it appears. The interpretation must be in harmony with the clear teaching on divorce and remarriage found elsewhere in the New Testament. And it must be made in light of the Jewish customs that handle pledging and marriage differently. This is how I believe the exception clause in Matthew 5:32 should be interpreted: But I tell you that anyone who divorces his wife, "except for immoral sexual behavior within the pledging period," causes her to become an adulteress, and anyone who marries the divorced woman commits adultery.

In addition to ignorance and misuse of the scriptures, Meaninglessness has played a significant role in many Christian's choice not to honor their marriage covenants. Meaninglessness allows people to treat their marriage covenant as if it never existed, as if the words were never uttered. Meaninglessness drains the meaning out of words.

For example, "Till death do we part" doesn't mean that we will stay together until we die. We say "till death do we part," but we mean something totally different. Those words may have meant "I'm going to stay married to you until one of us dies" a hundred years ago, maybe even sixty-five years ago, but they don't mean that today. The meaning shifted over time to "I'm going to stay married to you until we face difficult and painful circumstances."

It's kind of like two by four lumber. It used to be two inches wide and four inches high, but over time it magically shrunk. Now it is only three and a half inches by one and a half inches. It is still called a "two by four," but it is not two inches by four inches anymore. In case a storm blows through, I'd like to be in a house built out of real two by fours. And when a marital storm blows through, I'd like to be in a covenant marriage built out of real words that mean "Till death do we part." Where Meaninglessness exists, the wedding vows have also come to mean less and less. *Meaninglessness has damaged our most sacred words because we allowed it to spend time with our common words.*

I'll mention one other reason why Christians are ignoring their marriage covenants. It may be the most significant of them all. We'll talk about it in the next chapter.

Chapter 13
Self on the Cross or on the Run?

If anyone would come after me, he must deny himself and take up his cross daily and follow me. For whoever wants to save his life will lose it, but whoever loses his life for me will save it.
—Jesus (Luke 9:23–24)

I've lived a life that's full, I traveled each and ev'ry highway, And more, much more than this, I did it my way.
—Paul Anka

Paul Anka wrote *My Way* in 1969, and Frank Sinatra made a huge hit out of it. It was a wild year, a time of experimentation and social change. NASA's scientists were close to putting a man on the moon, but our politicians couldn't seem to get our men out of Vietnam. Bobby Kennedy and Martin Luther King were assassinated that year. And no-fault divorce debuted that year in California and spread like wildfire throughout the rest of the country. Divorce rates surged upward, and the Evangelical Church found itself yielding to these new pressures instead of opposing them. The age old standards for divorce and remarriage were quietly surrendered without a battle. And a generation of Christians hummed *My Way* with the radio during the week and sang *The Old Rugged Cross* on Sunday morning. They were confused, and many are still confused about whom to follow–Jesus or self–and who should go to the cross.

Following Jesus means self has to go to the cross. As Jesus said, "If anyone would come after me, he must deny himself and take up his cross daily and follow me" (Luke 9:23). Going to the cross is a frightening thought. And that fear, the fear of death to self, is the final cause I'll mention for why Christians choose not to honor their marriage covenants.

The cross presents a dilemma for a Christian reared in a *My Way* kind of world. He reads in his Bible that embracing the cross is the right thing to do, but it's hard to understand why, or even how to do it in a society that scoffs at that kind of thinking. Jesus commands him to lay down his life, but the world ridicules him if he doesn't stand up for his rights. The result is a confused double-mindedness that works in neither Christianity nor the world. As James said " . . . he is a double-minded man, unstable in all he does" (James 1:8). He is a man who is unable to embrace the cross, its pain as well as its resurrecting powers.

The cross is an unusual killing tool. Most instruments of execution simply take life, but the cross has the unique capacity to take life, exchange it, and then resurrect it at a higher level. As Paul said, "I have been crucified with Christ and I no longer live, but Christ lives in me . . ." (Gal. 2:20). Christians who run from the cross of a painful marriage cheat themselves out of this experience and in the process, experience all the painful consequences that follow those who break their marriage covenants.

Covenants take our old life, but they give us new life. In the covenant with Jesus, the believer is "crucified with Christ" but gains eternal life, the very life of Christ. In the covenant with our spouse "the two will become one flesh" (Eph. 5:31). Obviously, something's got to give a little when this happens. Like Siamese twins with different agendas, a little friction is inevitable any time two become one flesh without being one in spirit also. The something that must give a little, maybe a lot, is our self. Now I know that statement is heretical to a self-centered world or church, but it is still true. The *My Way* philosophy doesn't work so well when two become one flesh. What if both members of a couple are singing *My Way* at the same time? People who don't understand the seriousness of this process–the death of self–instinctively recoil from it as it begins to take effect. The fear of death of self keeps Christians from fully embracing their covenants with their spouse.

Covenants are like the stakes driven into the hands and feet of the condemned on the cross (I'll probably never write a romantic novel). They keep us pinned to the cross when everything in us yells

"Run for your life!" Our flesh prefers thumbtacks to railroad spikes just in case things don't work out so well. But it takes a covenant spike to hold us firmly to the cross, especially if marriage becomes our cross. It is a cross for many that results in the death of self. And it requires a death grip called covenant to hold the spouses in place on the cross until God works a miracle of resurrection in their marriage.

In my experience as a professional counselor, too many Christians in painful marriages today refuse to wait for God to do His work. They are paying close attention to the complaints of the flesh but ignoring their promises to God. They can't seem to forget their mate's harsh words, and they can't seem to remember their wedding vows. Why, you ask? Because we think like the world now. It is self-centered. Its words have become meaningless. It runs from its commitments. And it refuses to forgive.

But like Joe Lewis said of his fight with Billy Conn in 1946, "He can run, but he can't hide." We can run from the cross of a painful marriage, but we can't hide. To run from our cross is to run from Jesus. Christians who try to save their "lives" by running from a painful marriage often find that they have only exacerbated their problems. The escape from their cross leads to the imprisonment of an increasingly meaningless existence. For a Christian, a meaningful life is a life with Jesus. But Jesus said "If anyone would come after me, he must deny himself and take up his cross daily and follow me" (Luke 9:23). A paraphrase of the corollary to this verse would be something like this: If anyone chooses not to follow me, he will indulge himself and refuse to take up his cross daily.

CHAPTER 14
The Consequences of Broken Covenants

Instead of getting married again, I'm just going to find a woman I don't like and give her a house.
—Lewis Grizzard

Lewis Grizzard found a solution to his relational problems that seemed to work for him. This quote highlights one of the many consequences of divorce–everyone loses financially. In the article entitled "After the Split" Gene Meyer states "Let's be blunt: If you hire a divorce lawyer today, there is a good chance you will hire a bankruptcy lawyer within two or three years." The problems with finances, health, and relationships that follow a divorce have been thoroughly studied and are well-documented. What hasn't been thoroughly studied and would be more difficult to document, are the spiritual consequences of breaking a marriage covenant.

God uses Malachi to confront His people about the issue of broken covenants and to describe some of the spiritual consequences that follow a broken marriage covenant.

> You weep and wail because he no longer pays attention to your offerings or accepts them with pleasure from your hands. You ask, 'Why?' It is because the Lord is acting as the witness between you and the wife of your youth, because you have broken faith with her, though she is your partner, the wife of your marriage covenant (Mal. 2:13–14).

This passage was written sometime around 440 B.C. But God has not changed the way He looks at broken covenants in the past twenty-five hundred years. He looks at broken marriage covenants today the same way He looked at them in this passage from Malachi. "Jesus Christ is the same yesterday and today and forever" (Heb. 13:8). And people, whether they acknowledge it or not, experience the same consequences today that Malachi described above.

An observation of this passage reveals three key consequences the people experienced. First, they are sad about something; they are weeping and wailing. Secondly, and far more troublesome, is the fact that God is ignoring their best efforts to get His attention. Finally, they are confused. They have no idea why God is so upset. Malachi explains the reason why, one they had not considered prior to the confrontation: they broke faith with the wife of their marriage covenant. Although they had ignored and then broken their marriage covenant, God had done neither.

They ignored their covenant with the wife of their youth, and God responded accordingly, ignoring their efforts to embrace Him with their offerings. It's a two-way street, and God was sending a message through Malachi. Pay attention to your words of covenant if you want me to pay attention to your words of petition. Ignore your words of covenant without repentance, and I'll ignore your other words too.

The same problem is occurring in the Church today and in epidemic proportions. *The Church cries out in frustration for real revival, but God doesn't appear to be listening. Could it be for the same reason that He was not listening twenty-five hundred years ago?* His people have not changed all that much in twenty-five hundred years. They still ignore their covenants, and they still are surprised that it is a big deal to God. He stands ready to forgive every sin, but we need to repent.

How the people got so tangled up is really pretty simple to trace:

1. Breaking a covenant is a sin.
2. People deny and ignore this fact.
3. Therefore, they never confess the sin of covenant breaking.
4. The unconfessed sin breaks fellowship with God.
5. The broken fellowship creates a sense of alienation from God.

1. *Breaking a covenant is a sin.* Breaking a covenant is still a sin. It always has been and always will be. And like all other sin, it can be confessed and repented of. But something about covenant breaking makes it especially hard to acknowledge. Scripture records several instances in which the people who are confronted with the sin of covenant breaking are surprised by two things: God's displeasure and the intensity of His response.

In addition to the instance mentioned in Malachi, the thirty-fourth chapter of Jeremiah records a story that occurred during the Babylonian siege of Jerusalem in 588 B.C. . In all of Judah, only three fortified cities were still resisting the Babylonians, and the outlook behind the walls of Jerusalem was becoming increasingly bleak. In utter desperation, King Zedekiah made a covenant with all the people of Jerusalem to proclaim freedom for the slaves. These "slaves" were Israelites who were supposed to be set free after six years of service according to the Law; however, this right to freedom was often ignored by their greedy masters.

Maybe King Zedekiah was hoping to gain God's protection from the Babylonians by this act of obedience, or maybe he thought that the freed slaves would present a better defense against the Babylonians. Only God knows his motives, but we all know what happened next. The Israelites made a covenant with their slaves, guaranteeing them their freedom. They slaughtered a calf, cut it in two pieces, and then walked between the pieces indicating their willingness to be treated like the slaughtered calf if they broke their covenant with their slaves.

Not long after making this covenant, the Babylonian siege was temporarily lifted due to Egyptian intervention. And the Israelites went back to business as usual. They broke their covenant, and put their fellow Israelites back under bondage. God tested their integrity, and they failed. He then summoned the Babylonians back to Jerusalem in 586 B.C. to finish what they had begun–the complete destruction of the city.

This is what God told Jeremiah to tell the people who broke the covenant with their fellow Israelites:

> The men who have violated my covenant and have not fulfilled the terms of the covenant they made before me, I will treat like the calf they cut in two and then walked between its pieces. The leaders of Judah and Jerusalem, the court officials, the priests and all the people of the land who walked between the pieces of the calf, I will hand over to their enemies who seek their lives. Their dead bodies will become food for the birds of the air and the beasts of the earth. (Jer. 34:18–20)

Don't think for a minute that this was harsh or mean-spirited behavior on God's part. God was only doing what the slave holders requested He do as part of the covenant ceremony. Implied in the ceremony of covenant is the request that God do to them what they did to the calf if they broke their agreement. He granted their request.

Christians today, like the leaders of Jerusalem in the days of Jeremiah, want to believe that they can violate a covenant with their brothers and sisters without consequences. But God is still watching. He still considers covenant breaking a sin, and He still chastens his children.

The final example I'll mention of God's view of covenant breaking comes from Deuteronomy and deals with the land of Israel.

> All the nations will ask: 'Why has the Lord done this to this land? Why this fierce, burning anger?' And the answer will be: 'It is because this people abandoned the covenant of the Lord, the God of their fathers, the covenant he made with them when he brought them out of Egypt . . . ' (Deut. 29:24–25).

Something about the sin of breaking a covenant produces a "fierce, burning anger" in God but only a yawn of indifference in the men and women who break it. What is it about this particular sin that elicits such a different response from God and men? *It is the way we look at words.* God places the highest priority on them and holds His own in highest esteem. "[F]or You have exalted above all else Your name and Your word and You have magnified Your word above all Your name!" (Psalm 138:2b TAB). Some men don't look at their words like that. They forget they were ever uttered and are surprised that anyone, including God, would ever hold them accountable for what they said.

2. *People deny and ignore this fact.* People denied and ignored the fact that covenant breaking was a sin in Malachi's day, and they deny and ignore it today. The sin of covenant breaking creates some unique challenges for those caught in it, challenges that make it difficult to confess and forsake. But that is exactly what needs to happen.

3. *They never confess the sin of covenant breaking.* In both the Old and New Testament, God has made it clear that He will forgive His people when they confess their sin and turn from their wicked ways. But some sin is harder to confess than others.

What makes covenant breaking so difficult to deal with today is the fact that enormous efforts of justifying the decision to divorce have gone into the process. The sin is so disruptive to family life, and the practical consequences are so painful that it is the rare man or woman who says "I was wrong" after a divorce. Most have woven such a web of excuses around their decision to break their marriage covenant that saying "I was wrong" seems impossible. But it is truly repenting and saying "I was wrong" that restores fellowship with God and removes the sense of alienation.

4. *The unconfessed sin breaks fellowship with God.* "But your iniquities have separated you from your God; your sins have hidden his face from you, so that he will not hear" (Isaiah 59:2). Any unconfessed sin causes the sinner to drift away from God without being conscious of the process. When a person does not confess a sin they have committed, they will find themselves defending it. That's the way sin is. It must be flatly rejected, or the sinner will find himself defending it and then embracing it.

5. *The broken fellowship creates a sense of alienation from God.* Why is God ignoring these people's efforts to contact Him in Malachi? He is ignoring their words because they have ignored their covenant–the most sacred words of all. They forgot that God was there witnessing the sacred transaction called marriage. If people ignore what they say to God in a sacred covenant ceremony, why should He pay close attention to the more mundane words of praise and petition that they offer Him? That sounds only fair to me but harsh by today's standards. Actually, it's more than fair considering the fact that a mere mortal, dressed in his best suit, looks into the eye of God on his wedding day and makes a solemn vow to his wife that he chooses to ignore. If God wasn't so patient, it could be a lot worse. But our God is remarkably patient, and He stands ready to forgive us completely when we repent.

CHAPTER 15
Damage to the Godly Seed

Has not the Lord made them one? In flesh and spirit they are his. And why one? Because he was seeking godly offspring.

—Malachi 2:15

One of the consequences following covenant breaking is damage to the godly seed. When a couple splits, a family splits, and when a family splits, the children are split. Christians in miserable marriages don't want to think about this, but they should. Children will experience some very negative consequences when either or both of their parents choose not to love each other. Scriptural truth, recent scientific studies, and my own experience as both a counselor and a child of divorce validate this truth.

Scriptural truth indicates that covenant breaking damages the godly seed. The specific details of how the damage is done are omitted, but the fact that it occurs is undeniable. Malachi continues where I left off in the last chapter, "Has not the Lord made them one? In flesh and spirit they are his. And why one? Because he was seeking godly offspring. So guard yourself in your spirit, and do not break faith with the wife of your youth. 'I hate divorce,' says the Lord God of Israel," (Mal. 2:15–16a).

One of the reasons why God wants the covenant to remain intact is the fruit that it produces; "he was seeking a godly offspring." Something about divorce, and the remarriage that so commonly follows it, damages the children's capacity for godliness.

What does divorce do to children? In his article entitled "The Effects of Divorce on Children and Families," Dr. Tom E. Linaman catalogues a long list of problems that researchers found in the children of divorce. Dr. Linaman includes over thirty items on his list; I've picked a small sample to present here.

- After divorce, children tend to become more emotionally distant from both the custodial and non-custodial parent.
- As adults, children of divorced parents are half as likely to be close to their parents as are children of intact families.
- When the parents of both spouses have divorced, the risk of divorce is increased by as much as 620% in the early years of marriage, which declines to 20 percent by the 11th year of marriage.
- Adult children of divorced parents experience mental health problems significantly more often than do the adult children of intact families.

- Children whose parents divorce have lower rates of graduation from high school and college and also complete fewer college courses.
- Wallerstein found that 15 years after the divorce, only 10 percent of the children felt positive about it.
- *Following a divorce, children are more likely to stop practicing their faith.*

All of these problems are troubling, but according to Malachi 2:15, the last one on the list is the most disturbing to God. He's looking for godly offspring, but something about a broken covenant between a child's parents makes children less interested in the faith of their fathers. A 2001 study by L.E. Lawton and R. Bures published in the *Journal for the Scientific Study of Religion*, sheds some light on the subject. A synopsis of this research by Scott Stanley reveals that "children of divorce (whose parents divorced while they were children) are 62% more likely than children of non-divorced parents to no longer identify with the faith of their parents when they grow up." Catholics were 1.7 times as likely to switch to moderate Protestant denominations. Moderate Protestants were 2.6 times as likely to switch to conservative Protestant denominations and twice as likely to switch to Catholicism. But the highest switch factor of all belonged to conservative Protestants. After a divorce, their children were 2.7 times as likely to reject the faith altogether.

Rejecting faith altogether and divorce are

clearly associated, but why? What's the connection? The children are saying "what's important to you (your religious faith) is not important to me" because the parents said "what's important to you (keeping the family intact) was not important to me" years ago. The faith of their fathers was not strong enough to protect the most important thing in the world to the children–their family–and they have no use for it. This is a disaster because these kids are choosing to figure life out for themselves without the help of their father's Bible.

Or, maybe it's without the help of their stepfather's Bible. When parents choose to break their marriage covenants, children can lose both parents. The father is usually the first to go. He frequently plays a diminished role in their life, especially if a move occurs after the divorce. Although the mother usually retains custody and is there physically, her relationship with her children is often abruptly adjusted if she chooses to remarry.

Mom's new husband wants to know who comes first. "Is it me or your kids? Is it your kids or my kids?" While the new couple struggles to sift it all out, everybody suffers. Mom gets stretched like a rubber band. If she prioritizes her children, she can alienate her new husband. If she prioritizes her new husband, which is frequently the case, her children feel betrayed. The children lost their father when he found another woman, and they lost their mother when she found another man. As you can see, the children are the losers in the divorce and remarriage game. The divorce, which was supposedly for the benefit of the children, and the remarriage which so commonly follows it, produces a type of confused orphan. Both Mom and Dad are living, but their loyalties and priorities are elsewhere. This is very painful and very confusing for a child.

Another confusing problem for these children centers on the relationship with the step-parent. To embrace the step-parent is to be disloyal to the biological parent in the child's mind. "You took my father's place. If I choose to love you, I am not being loyal to my father." This dynamic is exacerbated by tension and hard feelings between their biological mother and father. It is a confusing and heavy burden that children were never meant to carry. This as well as other problems energize the fantasy in a child's mind that their parents will get back together. When their parents are separated, the children don't feel "together."

The final issue I'll mention is the self-centered orientation of the child. They believe that everything in life revolves around them. If their parents are angry, they think they have done something wrong. If their parents divorce, they think they are the cause. If they are ignored or rejected by the departing parent, they feel unworthy of love. They never think "I guess Dad's got problems of his own right now . . . He'll probably need a little time to work it out." They believe that it is all about them. Kids are resilient and can continue to function, but they are never the same after divorce. This is not academic for me–I lived it.

As a counselor, I've relived it too many times.

It's time for people who claim to know Jesus Christ as Lord and Savior to stop playing around and start honoring their marriage covenants, even when it hurts. That is how David describes those who wish to have access to God at His temple. They keep their oaths "even when it hurts" (Psalm 15:4). God can do miracles with miserable marriages (He did with mine). But too many of His children today are unwilling to hang around long enough to experience this.

Divorce is not the answer. Prayer, fasting, and a desperate cry to God for the desire to keep the covenant we no longer want to keep, to love the person we no longer want to love, that is the answer. Rather than run we begin to fight, not against our mate but against the forces trying to destroy our marriage. Our self-centeredness would be a good place to have the first battle, a battle of prayer and fasting, not of harsh words and hostility.

As a counselor exposed to the harsh realities of family violence, I know that some situations are dangerous. In the most severe cases, a woman and her children must literally run for their lives, or they will all be killed. If caught in that situation I too would run, remain single, and pray for a miracle. However, let me add, my intended audience is Christian. A man threatening to kill his family cannot legitimately make that claim. "The man who says, 'I know him,' but does not do what he commands is a liar, and the truth is not in him" (I John 2:4). God commands us to "Love one another" whether we feel like it or not

(John 13:34). How did we come to believe that obedience to that command was optional, that the words of Jesus could be ignored as if they had never been spoken?

Chapter 16
Exposing the Sin

An evil can seep through society so that even good people are blind to it. Then it is the responsibility of those who can see to speak out.
—William Lloyd Garrison

*O! what authority and show of truth
Can cunning sin cover itself withal*
—William Shakespeare

Exposing sin in the church today is a difficult proposition. Sin that has not been confronted for decades seems to cover itself, as Shakespeare said, with a sense of authority and a "show of truth," or legitimacy. Sin is a strange animal; when you ignore it, it thinks you accept it. Like a stray dog, sin makes your home its home unless you chase it away. Passive indifference looks like a "rooms available" sign to sin.

Liberalism's accusing finger has successfully intimidated the passive churches into saying "yes" to everything. Some denominations cannot even say "no" to homosexual clergy any more. Because of the inability to say no, the church has acquired too many strays. Our flower beds are dug up, our yards are full of poop, and the mail man doesn't even bother any more.

It reminds me of a true story that I heard firsthand from a Hindu monk, who I'll call "Vishnu." Vishnu lived in a teepee on a yoga commune. One evening he befriended a hungry raccoon and shared some food with it. The friendship grew, and his friendly little raccoon began to come inside the teepee for dinner every night. That raccoon brought another friendly little raccoon over for some free chow. Before long, there were four or five friendly adult raccoons coming into his teepee every evening for a handout. His meager food allowance was enough to help one, maybe two raccoons but not four or five.

One evening Vishnu finished feeding them and said, "That's it . . . that's all I have to give you tonight." That pack of raccoons inside the crowded teepee bared their teeth and began to growl at him. And he wondered for a moment if he would be their meal that night. Vishnu made a split-second decision that probably saved his life. He grabbed his wooden meditation elbow rest (almost as good as a baseball bat when you're in a pinch) and began to swing it wildly at the raccoons while yelling as loudly as he could. Thankfully, the raccoons chose to run instead of eating him for dinner that night. That's a strange thought–an animal eating a vegetarian for dinner. Seems a bit ironic, doesn't it?

That's how sin is. It seems friendly at first, but when it is allowed to grow, it becomes increasingly bold, demanding, and dangerous. The sin of covenant breaking and the adultery which so commonly follows it are no exception. It growls if we dare suggest, as Paul, that remarriage while a covenant partner remains alive is considered by God to be adultery. These sins are cheating the church out of the revival she craves, and it's time to expose them, confess them, and forsake them.

There aren't many sins that are easy to talk about anymore. Murder is a fairly safe target anywhere unless it involves unborn babies. Then care is required because recent estimates indicate that about one-quarter of church membership have been involved in an abortion in some way. Homosexuality is still a fairly safe target in most churches, but that is not true in some denominations any longer. Adultery is out of the question; too many church members are involved in this sin. Many of whom are only vaguely aware that they have done anything wrong.

The Evangelical Church no longer defines adultery as Paul defined it. Paul's definition continues to be the clear understanding in the Catholic Church as well as in the Bible believing Anglican Communion Network and Orthodox Churches, but it is no longer the standard for the Evangelical Church.

This is the standard that Paul set for the Church when he penned the book of Romans: "So then, if she marries another man while her husband is still alive, she is called an adulteress. But if her husband dies, she is released from that law and is not an adulteress, even though she marries another man" (Rom. 7:3). This is a simple and clear definition of what constitutes an adulterous relationship in the eyes of God. Unless God has changed His mind, He still considers it to be adultery when anyone marries a second or subsequent time when their original covenant partner remains alive.

Paul affirms the same teaching in First Corinthians that he put forth in Romans, "A woman is bound to her husband as long as he lives. But if her husband dies, she is free to marry anyone she wishes, but he must belong to the Lord" (I Cor. 7:39). Notice, it is not divorce that frees a person to remarry in the New Testament, it is death. These scriptures seem clear enough, but they appear to be ignored by the Evangelical Church today.

How could God be clearer than this? "To the married I give this command (not I, but the Lord): A wife must not separate from her husband. But if she does, she must remain unmarried or else be reconciled to her husband. And a husband must not divorce his wife" (I Cor. 7:10–11). Separation is addressed in this verse, but it is not the key issue. The key issue is that a separated (divorced) woman must remain unmarried or be reconciled to her husband. Why? Because when she marries another man while her husband is still alive, she becomes an adulteress. The same standard applies to a man who remarries while his covenant partner is still living. Death is the only way to terminate a marriage covenant in God's eyes. This is the standard of the New Testament, the new covenant.

This Biblical standard of what constitutes an adulterous relationship has been knocked off its supports much like the bar in the high jump pit at a track meet. The Evangelical Church is afraid to put it back in place because almost thirty percent of its couples can't clear this standard anymore. The bar must courageously and lovingly be put back in place.

Jesus replaced the bar to the high standard that God initially set. It was hardness of heart that knocked it off in the Old Testament, and it is hardness of heart that is knocking it off today. Jesus said "'For this reason a man will leave his father and mother and be united to his wife, and the two will become one flesh.' So they are no longer two, but one. Therefore what God has joined together, let man not separate" (Mark 10:7–9). This sounds clear enough to me, but it is not clear to many professing believers today. Jesus' stated desire for a couple not to separate is roundly ignored, rationalized and excused by the Evangelical Church today.

His clear teaching on adultery is likewise ignored by the Church in general. "He answered, 'Anyone who divorces his wife and marries another woman commits adultery against her. And if she divorces her husband and marries another man, she commits adultery'" (Mark 10:11–12). This scripture addresses both husband and wife. Some have said "Yes, but this applies only to those putting away and not the innocent victims of divorce."

The question of the innocent victim of divorce is addressed in the Gospel of Luke. "Anyone who divorces his wife and marries another woman commits adultery, and the man who marries a divorced woman commits adultery" (Luke 16:18). This "divorced woman" is a victim of divorce. She didn't initiate the process; yet, to marry her after her divorce is considered adulterous. Understanding covenant is the only way to make sense out of these scriptures. It's not as complex as people think. It's very simple in God's mind. When people enter a sacred covenant, they stay there. If they leave and remarry, regardless of how sweet and kind they are, they become adulterers and adulteresses.

The message of these six scriptures from Romans, First Corinthians, and the gospels of Mark and Luke are in perfect harmony, and they are crystal clear. But they are ignored today and stripped of their authority in favor of the two "exception clauses" discussed earlier in this book. Matthew, although not written to gentiles, is the first choice of gentiles when it comes to escaping a painful marriage.

That is amazing, isn't it? Multiple references by three different authors writing to gentiles are ignored in favor of two references written by a single author to Jews. How can that happen? Are these Christians truly searching diligently for God's will, or are they ignoring it? The flesh honors no command of our Lord Jesus Christ when struggling to catch its breath in a miserable marriage. The flesh needs to be crucified, but too many Christians refuse when it comes to divorce and remarriage.

Non-believers have complete freedom when it comes to covenant breaking and remarriage or any other sin for that matter. They claim no master and can behave as they see fit. Even Jews who continue to live under the Old Covenant of Law have much more freedom than Christians have. Jews can point to the book of Deuteronomy for an escape from a painful marriage. "If a man marries a woman who becomes displeasing to him because he finds something indecent about her, and he writes her a certificate of divorce, gives it to her and sends her from his house, and if after she leaves his house she becomes the wife of another man . . ." (Deut. 24:1–2). Freedom to remarry after divorce was present under the Law of the Old Testament.

But Christians are no longer under the Law of the Old Testament. We have entered a New Testament (Covenant) with Jesus Christ. Jesus is clear about why Moses allowed divorce.

> 'It was because your hearts were hard that Moses wrote you this law,' Jesus replied. 'But at the beginning of creation God "made them male and female." "For this reason a man will leave his father and mother and be united to his wife, and the two will become one flesh." So they are no longer two, but one. Therefore what God has joined together, let man not separate.' (Mark 10:5–9)

According to the Bible, something remarkable happens to the old stony heart when people enter the New Covenant with Christ, when they are born again.

"I will give you a new heart and put a new spirit in you; I will remove from you your heart of stone and give you a heart of flesh. And I will put my Spirit in you and move you to follow my decrees and be careful to keep my laws" (Ezek. 36:26–27). Divorce was permitted by Moses because of hard hearts, but according to this prophecy from Ezekiel, the excuse of a "hard heart" would vanish when a new heart and a new spirit would be placed within the believer in Christ. Christians are new creatures in Christ with soft hearts capable of working through this relational pain in the name and power of Jesus Christ.

Christ wants to leave this door open for reconciliation, but it is all too often prematurely slammed shut by remarriage to new partners. He wants us to fall on our knees in desperation and cry out for the grace to keep the covenant that we no longer want to keep, the grace to love the person that we no longer want to love. He wants us to tell Him the truth, "You'll have to love them through me because I can't do it, and I don't even want to anymore." This is the desire of Christ, but He doesn't get His way as much in the Church anymore. Christians like to sing about the old rugged cross, but they run from it if it shows up in their marriage.

Chapter 17
Why not Repent?

He who conceals his sins does not prosper, but whoever confesses and renounces them finds mercy.
—Proverbs 28:13

Some of the most rewarding times any parent will ever experience are tied to repentance. It feels so good for the wall to come down and to hear "Daddy, I'm sorry, I was wrong." Or, as is often the case in my home, me telling my children "I was wrong." What heart is not warmed by those words? What sin is too big to forgive when those words, sincere and heartfelt, come from one to another?

But some sin, based on the way we treat it, seems too big to forgive. After examining the sin of adultery and the silence surrounding it, it appears that many Christians secretly believe that the sin of adultery is unforgivable. Forgivable sin is discussed, repented of, and put away. But none of those things happen regarding divorce and adulterous remarriage within evangelical churches today. Discussing even the possibility that remarriage while the first mate remains alive is adulterous is completely taboo within evangelical churches. It wasn't for Paul when he wrote Romans and First Corinthians two thousand years ago, but it is for us today.

So what keeps Christians from discussing and repenting of the adultery which so commonly follows divorce within these churches today? Three things stand out as key obstacles: ignorance, fear, and pride. Let's start with ignorance. In 1940, divorce and remarriage were relatively rare. The standard was clearly set by the Church and upheld by family, friends, and the community–"You made your bed; you lie in it." But with the end of World War II in 1945, the sexual revolution of the sixties, and no-fault divorce taking root throughout the country in the early seventies, all that changed. By 1980 divorce rates soared to fifty percent for the first time in American history, and they have remained close to that figure ever since.

The social and relational pressures produced by these changes intimidated the Evangelical Church into silence on the issue of divorce and remarriage. People rarely respond well when confronted about their sin, but something about the sin of adultery seems to bring out the worst in us. After all, John the Baptist lost his head for confronting Herod Antipas about this sin. The truth troubled Herod, but it pushed his new wife, Herodias, to murder. To this day the words "it is wrong" still bother people who have not repented of this sin or any sin for that matter. No pastor will lose his head for saying those words today, but he may lose his job or a large part of his flock.

This intimidation and the resulting silence from the pulpit left Christians, who lacked the motivation to search out Biblical truth for themselves, completely unaware of what the Bible had to say about divorce and remarriage. The silence of Evangelicals led them to tacitly accept the practice of divorce and remarriage within the church. These powerful social pressures have all but eliminated the dissenting voice in evangelical churches to the practice of divorce and remarriage. With the disappearance of a dissenting voice, how would a church member who doesn't read his Bible know that marriage while a previous mate remains alive is considered to be adultery? And why would they ever see a need to repent? The topic is taboo–too emotionally charged to be put on the table for discussion.

In addition to ignorance, fear plays a key role in the silence. The uncertainty of how our loved ones will respond to the humble and risky choice to repent is a key factor in the process. The fear of rejection is very real and very intimidating for most of us. Not everyone will welcome the news that a Christian feels conviction that their choice to divorce and remarry was wrong, especially their new marriage partner. Fear of damaging an already fragile new union can keep people from bringing up this delicate topic.

The sin of adultery creates some unique and complex challenges for the man or woman entangled in it. *Adultery is one of the few sins that always implicate the partner.* People can rob a bank all by themselves, but adultery is hard to commit without a little help. If a Christian wants to confess and repent of adultery but their partner is not ready, they will have issues. The confession of one spouse places blame squarely in the lap of the other spouse also, blame they may not be ready, willing, or able to deal with. The less open and stable the new marriage, the less likely the issue will be put on the table.

An unrepentant spouse is not the only person who will have problems with a change of heart about this issue. In addition to the new spouse, family members and friends who supported the new marriage and hated the ex-spouse will not welcome the news that you have reconsidered your position on divorce and remarriage. Friends and family members who have divorced and remarried may not be eager to hear that you now believe that your choice, and by implication theirs too, was wrong. Yes, repentance is very risky and would take great courage to voice publicly, but that is exactly what needs to happen.

The fear of how repenting of divorce and an adulterous remarriage will effect people is very real. But how will it effect God? "How can I tell God that I'm sorry for being in an adulterous relationship and then stay in it?" "Would He take me seriously?" When children are conceived in the new marriage this question becomes even more perplexing. "If I leave this marriage I've broken another vow and left another child without an intact family . . . would God really want that? How do I make things right with God without making things wrong with my loved ones?" This is a difficult question, but I believe it has an answer, an answer that limits damage instead of creating more. We'll discuss it in the next chapter.

These fears form quite an obstacle for the child of God who is seeking renewed fellowship with Him, but pride is probably the biggest obstacle to true repentance. Saying "I was wrong" is one of the hardest things for a human being to do. Adam had trouble with it; he blamed Eve. Eve had some problems with it herself. And Christians still have trouble with pride today.

Saying "I was wrong" is always difficult, but saying it becomes much harder as the stakes rise. For example, Adam's sin caused terrible consequences that people around the world must face every day. For him to face humanity and say "I was wrong" would take great courage, especially facing those caught in the flames of hell. There could be a little push back there for him.

Saying "I was wrong" after observing the consequences of divorce and remarriage on the children would be very difficult to do. The children's relationship with both parents is changed through the divorce and remarriage process. That's what the research presented earlier shows, and that's what I experienced as a child of divorce. To look the children in the eyes and say "I was wrong" would take tremendous courage and humility. Much easier to pretend it never happened and go on with life. But that decision compounds the relational and spiritual consequences. That decision means that pride must muscle up to protect us from experiencing the pain that our disobedience has created for the ones we love. And that decision cheats a believer out of the intimate fellowship with God that they crave.

CHAPTER 18
How Can I Ever Untangle This Mess?

But Hezekiah prayed for them, saying, "May the Lord, who is good, pardon everyone who sets his heart on seeking God–the Lord, the God of his fathers–even if he is not clean according to the rules of the sanctuary."

—II Chron. 30:18–19

This is a good question. Some may be asking themselves this question after reading this book. Some Christians are in a second or third marriage with children from each marriage. There is no way to put it all back together in a nice neat package, even if all parties wanted to. It's a troubling dilemma.

How do believers caught in a tangled series of broken covenants followed by remarriage make things right with God? How do they honor their covenants without tearing their blended families apart? This question troubled me for years; I had no answer. I believe this question has an answer, but I want to state it as my answer so as not to presume upon God and His generous kindness to us all.

In First Corinthians, Paul states a clear truth "To the married I give this command (not I, but the Lord): A wife must not separate from her husband" (I Cor. 7:10). Paul is saying "this is not my command. It is the command of Jesus Christ." However, in I Corinthians 7:12 he used the parenthesis very differently: "To the rest I say this (I, not the Lord)." To paraphrase it, Paul is saying "Jesus didn't comment on this situation, but I believe that this is the best course of action under these difficult circumstances." Throughout this book, I have done my best to apply the inspired word of God to these issues. What follows is an idea based upon the difficult circumstances that the Church now finds herself in regarding marriage, divorce, remarriage, and adultery. This idea is based on a scriptural principle, but it is still just a man's idea. I want you to accept it or reject it in that light.

A passage in II Chronicles addresses a situation with a similar dilemma. Hezekiah found himself tangled in the problem shortly after becoming king. After sixteen years of King Ahaz, the nation was in disarray. When Hezekiah, his godly son, took the throne, things began to change. In fact, they changed so rapidly that no one was prepared for the great crowds that came from all over Israel to celebrate the Passover.

Although most of the many people who

> came from Ephraim, Manasseh, Issachar and Zebulun had not purified themselves, yet they ate the Passover, contrary to what was written. But Hezekiah prayed for them, saying, 'May the Lord, who is good, pardon everyone who sets his heart on seeking God–the Lord, the God of his fathers–even if he is not clean according to the rules of the sanctuary.' And the Lord heard Hezekiah and healed the people (II Chron. 30:18–20).

Just as Judah in the days of Ahaz, the Evangelical Church has gone through a long season of apathy and disobedience regarding how it views its marriage covenants. Even if Christians humbled themselves and repented, they face the same problem Hezekiah faced–he could not follow the rules even if he wanted to. Christian marriages, divorces and blended families cannot be "unblended," and the wrinkles cannot be ironed out. Christians need a pardon from God.

As in the days of Hezekiah, believers need to set their hearts on seeking God, and ask Him for a special pardon. The option is to deny the sin and continue sliding down the slippery slope, watching the generations that follow fall into the same traps because their spiritual ancestors would not humbly and openly confess their sin. There is a better way. As the scripture says, "He who conceals his sins does not prosper, but whoever confesses and renounces them finds mercy" (Prov. 28:13).

A friend saw this troubling bumper sticker

recently, "Focus on your own Family." Until Christian standards of righteousness exceed those of the world, we have no message that the world wants to hear. If the salt loses its saltiness, how can it preserve the world? "It is no longer good for anything, except to be thrown out and trampled by men" (Matt. 5:13). That is exactly what the world is doing to the Church today. The Church needs a new start and real redemption with God on this issue.

Chapter 19
Redemption

Create in me a pure heart, O God, and renew a steadfast spirit within me.
—David (Psalm 51:10)

P raise the Lord, God offers redemption to believers who sin. Any believer, at any time, guilty of any sin, can choose to turn back to God and experience His full and complete forgiveness. Although David committed adultery and then murder to cover his sin, he found full redemption with God. The 51st Psalm is David's road map to redemption.

Steps to Redemption:

1. Ask for mercy; make yourself completely defenseless before God. "Have mercy on me, O God . . ." (Psalm 51:1). Contrast this with how Adam responded when he was caught red handed, "The woman you put here with me–she gave me some fruit from the tree, and I ate it" (Gen. 3:12). Not only does Adam blame Eve, but he blames God for putting her there with him. His response could be paraphrased something like this: "I was doing fine before she came along God . . . without her around this never would have happened." Blaming others and minimizing the offense fall on deaf ears, but God will hear and respond to a simple, humble cry for mercy.

2. Ask for a complete cleansing from sin. "Wash away all my iniquity and cleanse me from my sin" (Psalm 51:2). Since the flesh works overtime at hiding sin, ask the Holy Spirit to expose it all. Then get out a pen and some paper and see what happens.

3. Acknowledge the wrong action specifically. "For I know my transgressions, and my sin is always before me" (Psalm 51:3). The sins of bitterness, hard-heartedness, and an unforgiving spirit in the offended mate are no better than the sins of the offender. If others have been affected by this sin, they should be addressed also. For example, "I was wrong to have divorced your mother, your son, your sister, etc . . ."

4. Acknowledge that the sin was directed primarily against God. "Against you, you only, have I sinned and done what is evil in your sight," (Psalm 51:4a). Although sin hurts others, it is primarily directed against God. The choice to ignore His clear command is sin. It says "I don't care what you said or what you want . . . I'm the boss, and I do things my way."

5. *Admit that the consequences of the sin are right, just, and fair–and that God is correct in applying them.* "[Y]ou are proved right when you speak and justified when you judge" (Psalm 51:4b). This is the key to true repentance–fully accepting the consequences of sin. David knew the devastating consequences of his sin when he wrote this. They were explained to him clearly by Nathan in II Samuel 12:10–14. David's repentance is full because he welcomes these painful consequences. He says that God was right to say what He said, that He was right when He spoke. David also says that God's judgment was correct because He was justified when He judged. David was not wiggling out of anything. That is the only way to find redemption with God–to stop wiggling.

    That is how parents know their children are truly repentant when they have to spank them. They stop wiggling. They take their discipline without complaint which clearly says, "I know I was wrong, and I deserve my punishment." Those words are heavenly words to both earthly and heavenly fathers. Those are the words that bring true redemption with God; they reflect a heart that is right with God.

6. *Acknowledge the filth of the tendency to sin.* David offers no effort to protect himself or his reputation in verses 5–7. The allusion to hyssop and water is a picture of himself as a leper before God, in need of the prescribed cleansing for the moral leper he had become.

7. Ask God to cleanse you. "Cleanse me with hyssop, and I will be clean; wash me, and I will be whiter than snow" (Psalm 51:7). Notice that he is not trying to cleanse himself. He wants God to wash him. Too often Christians try to wash themselves by minimizing the offense or blaming others, but it does not bring the fellowship they hunger for. Throughout this Psalm, the appeal from David is directed towards God: "blot out my transgressions . . . Wash away all my iniquity . . . cleanse me from my sin . . . Cleanse me with hyssop . . . wash me . . . blot out my iniquity . . . Create in me a pure heart . . . renew a steadfast spirit within me . . ." All these redemptive acts are the work of God. Self generated redemption is a form of self-righteousness. It is worthless.

8. Do not offer a substitute. "You do not delight in sacrifice, or I would bring it" (Psalm 51:16). Many Christians offer substitute sacrifices to God. They give themselves a "spanking." For some it is depression, for others it is martyrdom of some kind, some effort to pay the price for sin themselves. The price has already been paid by Jesus, and efforts to pay for it with substitute sacrifices do not please God or restore the broken fellowship with Him.

9. Offer the real thing–brokenness before God over the sin. "The sacrifices of God are a broken spirit; a broken and contrite heart, O God, you will not despise" (Psalm 51:17). God liked to see this in the Old Testament, and He still does. Broken, finished with "my way" and open to His way.

His way is the only way to genuine redemption, and the road is always open. Our sin is the only roadblock, and *all of it* is graciously removed with our humble confession. "If we confess our sins, he is faithful and just and will forgive us our sins and purify us from all unrighteousness" (I John 1:9). That's a wonderful promise, isn't it? But sadly, many Christians can't seem to embrace it.

Many cannot embrace the reality of redemption because they allow their guilty feelings to override God's promise of forgiveness. They believe that feelings trump words. This is not the case in God's economy. They don't understand what God's word means to Him. "[F]or You have exalted above all else Your name and Your word and You have magnified Your word above all Your name!" (Psalm 138:2, TAB). They don't understand that He has exalted His word above all else. They can't fathom how important God's words are to Him.

Those who don't understand the impeccable integrity in God's character can't seem to embrace His redemptive promises. They can't seem to believe Him or hold on to His promises. The pollution of so many meaningless words makes their heart unable to believe and then attach itself to the truth. Much like a lint roller that's full of lint, it can't seem to grab anything else. No matter how much pressure is applied, no matter how badly you want it to, it just won't attach itself to anything when it's full of dirt.

Our hearts are the same way.

The desire to experience God's forgiveness, coupled with the inability to sense a connection with Him, creates a confusing sense of rejection that is almost palpable for some. I've felt that before, and I felt it most profoundly when my words were the most meaningless. Over the past eighteen years, the Great Physician has been treating my own case of Meaninglessness with His word. As my symptoms have gradually faded, I've found that His promise of forgiveness has become increasingly real to me. As my words have become increasingly meaningful, I've found that God's words have undergone a similar transformation.

Sadly, for many, the wonderful words of forgiveness and redemption that John penned above carry no more meaning than their own words. That's the final curse of Meaninglessness that I'd like to discuss. I've explained how Meaninglessness generates lies and empty words, how it damages relationships and creates problems with self-control. I've discussed why God doesn't listen to us when we're using meaningless words. I've said a lot about how Meaninglessness affects our words but not much about what it does to God's words.

We are hard wired to believe that God takes His words no more seriously than we take our own. It's a curse that keeps us from experiencing the sense of full redemption with God that our souls crave. We think God is like us. For example, if we are unforgiving, we think He is too. We would never say that in

Sunday school, but we will sense that our sins have not been washed away if we refuse to forgive others.

David makes this point in the 18th Psalm. "To the faithful you show yourself faithful, to the blameless you show yourself blameless, to the pure you show yourself pure, but to the crooked you show yourself shrewd" (Psalm 18:25–26). Would it be too big of a stretch to say, "To those who don't value their words, He appears not to value His words"?

Those that are unable to attach meaning to their own words are also unable to attach meaning to God's words. They know they should, but they can't. They can give the right answers to questions about God's goodness and mercy in Sunday school, but they can't feel it. It doesn't seem real to them. It's a problem of the heart, a problem I call "meaningless word buildup." It keeps the heart from being able to experience the truth fully. It's a serious and frustrating problem. But it is a problem that God can fully repair.

Meaninglessness and its consequences have been a part of the world since the fall of man. But over the past sixty years Meaninglessness has spread rapidly, virtually undetected, into our words. This epidemic moved from the world into our sanctuaries and has become a significant threat to the health of the Church. But the good news is that a cure is available.

The cure is repentance. Repenting always precedes redemption. Repenting means changing our minds about how we view our words and the covenants they establish. It means watching our words like a hawk. Repenting includes teaching our children about covenants and the importance of honoring their words. Our children need this inoculation to protect them from the disease of Meaninglessness.

In closing, my hope is that this book will encourage you to keep your covenants even when it hurts. Note that Psalm 15:4 says "when it hurts" not "if it hurts." Promises, vows, and covenants are made precisely for that reason, from time to time it hurts to keep them. Keeping these agreements always involves a cost.

Keeping our covenant with Jesus will cost us the right to maintain sovereign control of our life. Keeping our marriage covenant will cost us the freedom to terminate the relationship. Both of these covenants place significant restrictions on personal freedoms, and neither covenant should be entered into lightly. Both covenants take our life and yet give us so much more. These fears about losing the old lifestyle and freedoms need to be addressed prior to making life-changing covenants, not afterwards. Fear is not such a bad thing. My prayer is that Christians will once again learn to fear the Lord, paying close attention to what He says to them as well as what they say to Him.

Finally, I hope you never face a day like you imagined in the Introduction to this book, a day in which words loose their meaning. But if you do, you'll know what happened, why it happened, and just what to do. May God bless you and protect you from Meaninglessness, my friend.

BIBLIOGRAPHY

Akin, Jimmy. "Did Jesus Say Adultery is Grounds for Divorce?" *Catholic Answers.* Vol. 11. 7–8. July 2000. <http://www.catholic.com/thisrock/2000/0007bt.asp>.

Bartlett, John. *Bartlett's Familiar Quotations: A Collection of Passages, Phrases, and Proverbs Traced to Their Sources in Ancient and Modern Literature.* 1855. Ed. Justin Kaplan. New York: Little, Brown and Company, 2002.

Betrothal, The Jewish Encyclopedia. Ed. Singer, Isidore. 3rd ed. New York: Funk and Wagnals Company, 1907. 126–26.

Dean, Bill. *I Am a Survivor.* Kearney, Nebraska: Morris Publishing, 2003.

Favorite Quotes on Divorce Reform. Americans for Divorce Reform. <http://patriot.net/~crouch/quotes.html>.

Lawton, L. E., & Bures, R. "Parental Divorce and the 'Switching' of Religious Identity." *Journal for the Scientific Study of Religion* 40, (2001): 99–111.

Linaman, Todd, E. "The Effects of Divorce on Children and Families." *Family Life Facts* (2005): <http://www.flc.org/hfl/marriage/mar-flf03.htm>.

Loftus, Elizabeth F. and Kethcham, Katherine. *The Myth of Repressed Memory: False Memories and Allegations of Sexual Abuse.* New York: St. Martin's Press, 1996.

Murray, Andrew. *The Two Covenants: Eighteen Meditations.* Ed. Robert Delancy. Fort Washington, Pennsylvania: CLC Publications, 2001.

Precept Ministries International. *Covenant: Precept Upon Precept.* Chattanooga, TN: Precept Ministries International, 2002.

Showers, Renald. http://www.biblestudymanuals.net/jewish_marriage_customs.htm>.

Sider, Ronald, J. "The Scandal of the Evangelical Conscience: Why Don't Christians Live what They Preach." *Christianity Today.* January/February 2005: <http://www.christianitytoday.com/bc/2005/001/3.8.html>.

Strong, James. *The Exhaustive Concordance of the Bible.* McLean, Virginia: Macdonald Publishing Company.

Trumbull, H. Clay. *The Blood Covenant: A Primitive Rite and its Bearings on Scripture.* Kirkwood Missouri: Impact Christian Books Inc., 1998.

Vine, W.E., Unger, M.F., and White, W. *Vine's Expository Dictionary of Biblical Words.* New York: Thomas Nelson Inc., 1985.

Zodhiates, Spiros, *The Complete Word Study New Testament.* Chattanooga, TN: AMG Publishers, 1992.

Zodhiates, Spiros, *The Complete Word Study Old Testament.* Chattanooga, TN: AMG Publishers, 1994.

About the Author

Tim Coody, his wife Laura, and their two children, Hannah and Katherine, live in a small community in East Texas. Tim received his Masters Degree in Professional Counseling from the University of Texas at Tyler in 1991 and has worked as a Licensed Professional Counselor for the past twelve years. Tim's background includes military service as a Marine helicopter pilot, as well as extensive domestic and international travel as a speaker-trainer in the medical field.

TATE PUBLISHING, LLC

127 East Trade Center Terrace
Mustang, Oklahoma 73064

(888) 361 - 9473

Tate Publishing, LLC

www.tatepublishing.com